THE
FINE ART
OF BEING
IMPERFECT

*And Other Broadcast Talks
from R. Maurice Boyd*

D1440937

ABINGDON PRESS
NASHVILLE

THE FINE ART OF BEING IMPERFECT
AND OTHER BROADCAST TALKS

Copyright © 1998 by Abingdon Press

This book is printed on recycled, acid-free, elemental-clorine–free paper.

Library of Congress Cataloging-in-Publication Data

Boyd, R. Maurice, 1932–
    The fine art of being imperfect: and other broadcast talks/from
R. Maurice Boyd.
        p.   cm.
    ISBN 0-687-45909-5 (alk. paper)
    1. Meditations.   I. Title.
BV4832.2.B685   1998
242—dc21

                                                                    97-49916
                                                                    CIP

98 99 00 01 02 03 04 05 06 — 10 9 8 7 6 5 4 3 2 1
MANUFACTURED IN THE UNITED STATES OF AMERICA

To the Governing Board
and
the Members and Friends
of
The City Church, New York

*Oh, these humans . . . knew how to dream
and did not need to fall asleep first.*

—Friedrich Nietzsche

CONTENTS

PREFACE
FOR YOUR EARS ONLY

John Rochford, of WQXR-FM, New York, the Classical Music Station of *The New York Times,* who produced and recorded these talks for radio, has been in the business of broadcasting for most of a lifetime, and is wise and experienced enough to distinguish between things that differ.

One thing he is sure of is the difference between doing things on the radio and using radio to do things. He likes the latter better, so it makes his day when the message is well-suited to the medium and makes the most of radio's distinctive qualities and unique opportunities.

I wish all who try to communicate were as astute as he is and as clear about what they are doing. Preachers, for example, should know the difference, both in form and intention, between a sermon and a lecture and between a written word and a spoken one. They should also be aware that a sermon in print is hardly a sermon at all, and one that is broadcast as it was preached in a church service is an invitation to hear by overhearing.

Broadcast talks should be intimate, as radio is, for they speak, not to the many, but to the one. Radio is as boundless as one's imagination. If you think these messages are for your ears only, and agree with the little girl who said she liked radio better than television "because the scenery is better," you have both recognized the nature of radio and understood what I was trying to do.

Recorded music was woven into the fabric of each broadcast, not only to allow listeners some respite from the spoken word, but also to enhance the claim of truth by the appeal of beauty. For beauty has its own authority. Some of our most cherished visions are believed because they are "too beautiful to be untrue."

The music was neither announced nor described, for there is a difference between a disc jockey and a preacher, even when they work out of the same studio.

The broadcasts were a gift to the City of New York from The City Church, New York, at an hour on Sunday morning when most New Yorkers were still in bed. The talks offered no information about the church, not even an address or telephone number; and they asked nothing of the listeners but their attention. This was mystifying to some, but the discerning knew what we were about and were reassured to discover that we knew the difference between a gift and a commercial. The recognition of limits is, after all, the soul of respect.

The broadcasts were made possible by the initiative and generosity of Bob and Dorothy Goldbach, who wanted the whole world to hear their preacher; and Pat Tretout exercised a kind of tender tyranny in steering the talks from the radio station to your local bookstore.

But my deepest debt of gratitude is to the Governing Board and the Members and Friends of The City Church, New York, a congregation I'd like to take on the road. By their humor, wisdom, and grace they make it the joy of my life to be their minister.

R. Maurice Boyd
The City Church, New York
Easter, 1997

1

ON NOT
MISSING GOD

*Do you know anyone who knows you better
than you know yourself?*

I saw *An Affair to Remember* at an impressionable age and have not been able to forget it. I especially remember how the lovers, played by Cary Grant and Deborah Kerr, missed each other between the east side of Fifth Avenue and the top of the Empire State Building. No happy ending could assuage the anguish of that. How unbearably poignant it is when those who love each other miss each other.

It can easily happen—all it takes is a head not turned or a face not lifted; a telephone not answered; a word not spoken, or not spoken in time; a letter not delivered—and the remnant of life becomes an inconsolable longing.

It happened to a man I knew years ago who forgot that "faint heart never won fair lady" and said nothing when he should have said something, so that the woman he loved grew weary of waiting and married somebody else. He never got over it. Having missed his heart's treasure, nobody else would do.

Saint Augustine tells us that something like that happened to him and God. He writes in his *Confessions:* "God was inside me. But I was outside myself. And that is how we missed each other." We know that the *Confessions* come to a satisfying end and that those who missed each other did not lose each other, but any words that speak of missing God leave the soul stricken and the heart faint. What did Augustine mean by them?

"God was inside me," he tells us, acknowledging right away that their missing each other was not God's fault but his own. He knew where God could be found even while he missed Him.

Augustine was more astute than we are. Like every high-school atheist, we miss God because we think He is outside us: an object among other objects, another being among all the beings in the world. We then debate whether or not we believe in Him, making Him a toy in our discussion, a plaything for our cleverness whose very existence hangs upon our arguments and depends upon our brilliance. We don't realize that by placing God outside us we have already taken the first step toward unbelief, for the God whose reality we try to prove does not exist.

Our debating the existence of a God outside us makes about as much sense as Prince Hamlet, King Lear, the Moor of Venice, and General Macbeth debating the existence of Shakespeare and attempting to settle the matter by discovering him among the characters in his plays. Shakespeare cannot be found in that way, for he does not exist in that way. He is not among the characters; he is in the characters, or the characters are in him, for they are his creation. Their connection with the one they seek is more intimate than they could ever imagine. He is the eyes of their seeing, the mind of their thinking, the heart of their loving, for "it is in him that they live and move and have their being."

It is like that with God, says Augustine. We cannot keep Him out, or push Him away, or hold Him at arm's length, for the strength of our arm is the force of His life in us. Whether or not we miss Him we cannot know ourselves apart from Him, for our knowing is the gesture of His presence. George MacDonald put it perfectly when he said that to present a far-distant God is the most absurd of all teachings. Either there is no God, or He is closer to us than our deepest awareness of self.

How shall we deny to God an intimacy everywhere visible? In love's philosophy nothing is single or separate; for the earth kisses the heavens and the sea the shore, the wind is the air of our nostrils, and starlight a region of our spirit. And God, the Country of our soul, is "closer to us than breathing and nearer than hands or feet."

We have spoken of intimacy, but we should recognize the degrees of it. Why, it ranges all the way from the most rudimentary knowledge of another to a kind of mystical union with another. If we are no longer satisfied to place God outside us, how are we to think of His presence within us?

We might well begin with Cole Porter, who not only knew what we are talking about, but also put it into words and set them to music. You must have heard Ole Blue Eyes singing in "I've Got You Under My Skin":

> I've got you deep in the heart of me.
> So deep in my heart, you're really a part of me.

Now, that's not a bad description of God's indwelling. It is what we mean when we speak of God's Spirit, for the Spirit is God under our skin. God's intimacy with us is the affinity of kindred spirits.

Kindred spirits may be closer to us than we are to ourselves. Don't you remember when you were in danger of losing yourself, someone who loved you refused to give you up or let you go? You now know that your faithfulness is their gift and your constancy their accomplishment, for they protected you when you were prepared to surrender and defended your center when you were ready to yield:

> Because of your firm faith I kept the track; I could not meet your eyes if I turned back,
> So on I went.

We cannot deny to our Creator a degree of intimacy enjoyed by a fellow creature. MacDonald is certain that if God exists at all we are more present to Him than we are to ourselves. That makes sense. Who is closer to Hamlet—Hamlet or Shakespeare? Who is more intimately acquainted with Dr. Faustus—Faustus or Christopher Marlowe who created him? It is in this way that God is present in His whole creation, making and remaking it from within. He knows it better than it knows itself.

We sometimes imagine that to pray to God is like going to a busy bake shop where every customer has to take a number and wait to buy bread. But we do not have to take our turn or wait or compete for God's attention, for we already have it—all of it, all the time. He is inside us and knows us from within. There is no instant when we are not entirely present to Him and no fragment of time when we slip out of His thoughts. As the psalmist says, such knowledge is too wonderful for us; but it is precisely what we mean by Infinite Mind.

The Apostle Paul describes this Divine intimacy with enormous tenderness when he says that God knows us at the depth of our inarticulate groans. Groans are inarticulate because they are wrung from us when we cannot think or understand or utter what we feel. Our sighs, like our tears, begin where our words leave off. Our groaning expresses what is beyond expression.

I heard a woman groan once, and have never forgotten it. She was saying good-bye to her son, whom she did not expect to see again this side of heaven; and all she could do was hold him with all the love of her heart and all the sorrow of the world, and groan her anguish.

At that depth, says the Apostle, God intercedes for us, pleads for us, speaks with the voice we cannot find, comforting us with His assurance that when we do not know, we are known; when we cannot understand, we are understood; when we cannot accept, we are accepted; when we cannot love, we are loved. He

The Fine Art of Being Imperfect

embraces what we are unable to express and interprets us to ourselves.

I read of a prayer convention held in London's Royal Albert Hall in the thirties and attended by thousands of believers from all over the world. An unforgettable prayer was offered by an old Scot. It began slowly, but as it continued it gained eloquence and depth. The man was carried beyond himself, discovering thoughts greater than his own thoughts and offering them in words better than his own speech. Then he began to lose it, being so far out of himself that he could no longer express what he felt or tell what he knew. Stammering to the edge of incoherence, he ended, "Lord, take the meaning! Take the meaning!" God always does, for He knows our meaning with a lover's intimacy.

"God was inside me," wrote Augustine, "but I was outside myself. And that is how we missed each other."

What did he mean when he spoke of being outside himself? How can you be outside of yourself; and if it is possible at all, what self is out and what self is left?

Frank O'Connor, who wrote the best short stories in the world, tells of a friend, a priest, he knew in Ireland. When the priest was a theological student, his mother suggested they might spend a Saturday afternoon together; but he refused her, saying that he was too busy with his studies, and went off to enjoy himself among his friends.

Imagine his embarrassment when he ran into his mother on the street. He began to stammer his excuses and offer his apology, but she cut him off: "Don't say anything," she told him, "for you have no word." To have no word is to be out of character, outside yourself, your true and inmost self, your own self, the self Whitman called "thou actual me."

The young Augustine was outside himself when he left home for Carthage, Rome, and Milan, to escape the watchful eye of his mother and, in love with loving, to indulge his passionate temperament and sensual nature. In his own far country he explored the heresies of the age, and in his own words, "scratched the itch of lust." He not only became a master of rhetoric, contemptuously describing himself as "a vendor of words," but also was appointed to the chair of rhetoric in the University, his "chair of lies," as he called it.

But Augustine began to miss God in a quite different way, for he began to long for God. Life-weary at thirty he cried, "Will I never cease setting my heart on shadows and following a lie?" He now sought God with the same fervent temperament and passionate intensity that had first caused him to miss God. Yearning, sighing, and thirsting for the spring of the Eternal Country, he discovered the truth of his own later words: "Thou hast made us for Thyself, O God, and our hearts are restless till they rest in Thee."

When Elgar wrote his *Enigma Variations,* he set himself—and some of the people he loved—to music. Each variation is unique, as it must be if it is to capture the individuality of each of his friends. But the "enigma" of the variations is more mysterious even than the personalities. It is another theme, played but not heard, overarching all the variations, gathering them into a harmony of a higher kind, and making the work complete.

Augustine would have thought Elgar's "enigma" but another name for "a divinity that shapes our ends, rough-hew them how we will"; for all that he had learned in Carthage, Rome, and Milan became grist for his mill. When at the age of forty-three he was elected Bishop of Hippo, he was uniquely equipped to salvage from a world in ruins the faith that was to become the foundation of a new civilization.

It seems that the longest way round is often the shortest way home and that it is sometimes impossible to separate our wanderings from our destiny.

I once met a woman who was eager to share with me her experience of Christian conversion. Authentic enough in itself, it had unfortunately led her to regard with contempt everything else that had ever happened to her. Hers was not the "tender contempt" with which we should all learn to regard the unhappy memories that return to torment us in the wee small hours, but an active hatred of forty years of a mixed but useful life.

Augustine was wiser than that. He wrote,

> I no longer wished for a better world because I was thinking of the whole creation, and in the light of this clearer discernment I have come to see that *though the higher things are better than the lower, the sum of all creation is better than the higher things alone.*

Of course there are no good bits and bad bits, only good and bad joined inextricably in this self I am. Do you not know that my gifts are my limitations; that my tenderness is inseparable from my frailty, my compassion from my failings, my insight from my sins, my understanding from my weakness?

This is the supreme accomplishment of the God who is, if anything, "too instant to be known"; who is inside us when we are outside ourselves, who silently moves the play and focuses its various parts, as John Moffit wrote in "Presence":

> Fashioning for the world and me,
> A wholeness from our opposites.

2

THE ROAD NOT TAKEN

*Do you ever compare the road you took
with the road you didn't take?*

Did you hear of the man who used to think he was indecisive, but now is not so sure? Robert Frost had a friend like that. He seemed incapable of making up his mind about anything, to the great amusement of the small group of poets to which they both belonged.

Just for the fun of it, Frost wrote a poem about the man's waffling; but when he read it to the company of poets, he was astonished to discover that they found it no laughing matter. They were not amused, but deeply moved, by the poignancy of his words.

He tried his joke again, on a gathering of university students this time, and received the same response. They, too, missed his humor but were touched by his tenderness. "The Road Not Taken" thus became the joke nobody caught, and one of Frost's best-loved poems.

Written in old England, the poem is set in New England, in New Hampshire's yellow woods where two roads branch off in different directions, forcing a traveler to choose between them. It ends by telling us that the poet

> . . . took the one less traveled by,
> And that has made all the difference.

Frost's choice was between writing poetry and teaching school; but in every life there are roads that diverge, beckoning this way or that, inviting us here or there. And that means indecision and decisions with their inevitable consequences of gladness or regret.

There is no avoiding them. Yogi Berra's alleged direction, "When you come to the fork in the road, take it," is both funny and futile. Not all dilemmas can be melted into an accommodating both/and; the stronger and more interesting ones claim to be either/or. They keep their jagged edges, resist all attempts at consensus, preserve their irreconcilable differences, and retain a bloody-minded insistence that we choose between them.

When we do choose, our decision may prove to be of the happiest sort; for the road taken may become the high road of adventure, opportunity, and fulfillment. But not all choices are like that. Some turn out badly. Hope deferred, or disappointed altogether, makes the heart faint. We blame ourselves for our distress and are tormented by our own reiterated, merciless, and unanswerable, "If only!"

When we behave like this, we are often less than fair. We punish ourselves more harshly than we deserve or the facts warrant. When our high hopes have sunk to a low mood, it is easy to forget what ought to be remembered for the strengthening of our courage and the renewal of our spirit.

We forget, for example, that while life must be lived forward it can only be understood backward. This observation, made by Søren Kierkegaard, reminds us that we should not judge our past choices as though we knew as much then as we do now. In the light of present experience we may reckon an earlier decision a poor one; but we did not have present experience when we made it. Knowing what we now know, we might have acted differently; but we didn't know what we now know when we acted. Hindsight is a valuable commodity, but it is not available when what we are attempting is foresight, and it is silly and hurtful of us to judge ourselves as though it were.

Speaking of his younger days, which, like ours, had their foolish mistakes and insensitivities, Dennis Potter said that he had come to regard them with "tender contempt." That phrase is memorable in its frankness and gentleness. Neither sentimental nor despairing, it invites us to appraise ourselves with both candor and kindness. The contempt is easy; it is the tenderness that is hard.

Not long ago, a friend told me that she had reread a book and that there was more in it the second time. I understood what she meant, but what she said was not true. There was not more in it than before. The book was exactly the same. Nothing had been changed or added. What she meant was that there was more in her when she read it a second time. Those who are quick to tell us that the Bible is irrelevant are often saying more about themselves than they are about the Scriptures. If I found the Bible irrelevant, it is not the Bible I'd be concerned about.

Truth is not a bit of stuff that lies around waiting to be picked up by the idly curious; it demands something of us before it will give itself to us. Schubert's songs will not surrender their secrets to the superficial; they require more than a pretty voice and an adequate technique. Singers should not rush to Richard Strauss's *Four Last Songs* or hasten to Mahler's *Song of the Earth* lest it be said of them, "Thou hast nothing to draw with, and the well is deep." Such music is inaccessible except to the committed. It asks of us a certain height, or depth, even to listen to it.

That is why we say, "You can't put an old head on young shoulders." Yet we blame ourselves as though we can. Should we feel guilty, then, that we know more at fifty than we did when we were twenty, or that we can grow a little wiser in any good year?

The Fine Art of Being Imperfect

We might heed another bit of homey wisdom and not allow our regret for what might have happened to spoil our appreciation of what did happen.

We are all guilty of it. George Orwell knew what he was talking about when he said that every life, viewed from within, is a series of defeats. Some of us insist on defining ourselves by our defeats—by all the things we have not done. Our glass is never half full, but always half empty. Nothing we have accomplished appears in any way significant when compared with what we have failed to accomplish. We allow our failures to add up to failure, our losses to make us losers, our defeats to defeat us, and ourselves to be diminished by the guilt and inferiority of our "might have been." Because we have not performed perfectly, nothing we have ever done has been any good.

When Elgar finished *The Dream of Gerontius,* he wrote at the end of the score a quotation from John Ruskin:

> This is the best of me. For the rest, I ate and drank and slept and loved and hated like another. But this I saw and knew; this if anything of mine is worth your memory.

But *Gerontius* is not the only bit of Elgar worth remembering. It may be the best of him, but his second or third or tenth best is still worth listening to. Yet in every record store there are discs for sale offering us "the best" of Beethoven or the "greatest hits" of Brahms or Sibelius. We are so competitive we make our musicians compete not only against one another, but against their own music.

Yet, as Chesterton loved to say, the best of us is only a very small part of us, and if a thing is worth doing, it is worth doing badly. Only trivial enterprises can be perfectly achieved. Artur Schnabel said he played only music that is better than it can be played. If I preached only when at my best, I might show up six times a year. Besides, we don't know we're at our best until afterward.

Even if we could accomplish everything perfectly, our lives would still not be perfect, for we cannot escape their unfinished-ness. Sir John Barbirolli and André Previn were once passengers in an aircraft caught in a violent thunderstorm. When it appeared that they would not survive, "Glorious John" was not terrified but outraged. Did the God of thunderstorms not understand that he had begun a new cycle of recordings and wished to finish it? Reinhold Niebuhr, in "The Irony of American History," wrote:

> Nothing that is worth doing can be achieved in a lifetime, therefore we must be saved by Hope. Nothing which is true or beautiful or good makes complete sense in any immediate context of history, therefore we must be saved by Faith. Nothing we do, however virtuous, can be accomplished alone, therefore we are saved by Love.

Jussi Björling, who died suddenly of a heart attack when he was in his prime, made several superb operatic recordings with Victoria de los Angeles. After his death, someone lamented to her that their plans to record *Manon* and *Otello* had come to nothing. She replied, "We must not spend time in regret over what we did not do, but be happy for what we did."

To compare the road we took with the road not taken is no fair comparison. It is to compare the actual with the ideal, the real with the fanciful, the defined with the unlimited, the factual with the fantastic, the definite with the unspecified, and the particular with a whimsical world of dreams.

We insist on doing it, though, especially when we are unhappy and filled with melancholy. Then we imagine our world as it would have been if we had done this instead of that, gone there instead of coming here, married this one instead of that one. We dream a world free of all the limitations of the world we know, including our own.

The Fine Art of Being Imperfect

It is a harmless enough game to play so long as we remember that it is a game. No one need deprive us of our daydreams or strip us of our fantasies so long as we are aware that we are dreaming and that our fantastic weavings are gossamer.

I sometimes write a fictional autobiography telling the story of what would have happened to me if I had not left Ireland nearly forty years ago. I have no doubt that I should have become Prime Minister. Northern Ireland is a small country, where they used to say that everybody knows somebody who knows the Prime Minister. At the very least I should have been made President of the Church there, for that happened to all my friends, and I was brighter and more virtuous than any of them.

In my fantasy it matters not a whit that I never wanted to be president of anything, or that I think politics should work like a good digestion—the less we are aware of it, the better. This is a fictional biography in which I can become anything I please, even something I have no wish to be.

The truth is, of course, that the day after I didn't leave Ireland, I could have been knocked down by a lorry, or struck by a terrorist's bullet, or drowned while bathing. Once we leave what actually did happen, we have no way of knowing what would have happened.

When we compare the road not taken with the road taken, we do ourselves a grave disservice; for it is this road on which we now travel that deserves our attention, and the dear people we meet on it who have a rightful claim to our devotion. The tomorrow we hope to enjoy cannot begin on a road we never took. Tomorrow may be another day, but its sun rises on the path now under our feet.

Someone once drew a line on a page and said the line was his life. He then drew other lines across it and said that where they crossed was where God had come in.

I think he was mistaken, for the truth is better than that. God cannot come in, for He was never out. If our life is a line drawn on a page, then God is the page on which it is drawn. There is no point of place or time in which the Divine Life does not impinge upon our own. Dame Julian of Norwich knew this when she said that we are all in Him enclosed, for He holds us in His hands. As Haskins wrote:

I said to the Man who stood at the gate of the Year, "Give me a light that I may tread safely into the Unknown."

And he replied, "Go out into the darkness and put thy hand into the hand of God. That shall be to thee better than light, and safer than a known way."

So I went forth, and finding the hand of God, trod gladly into the night. And He led me toward the hills and the breaking of day in the lone East.

The Fine Art of Being Imperfect

3
PSALMS AND SONGS

*Have you learned to see **through,** not **with,** the eye?*

Dennis Potter wrote some of the best plays ever written for television. You may recognize their names before that of their author: *The Singing Detective; Pennies from Heaven; Those Blue Remembered Hills,* and his last two, *Karaoke* and *Cold Lazarus,* which he finished just before he died in 1994.

One of the most interesting features of his plays is that, though he never wrote a musical, he utilizes popular songs to enhance the events. It can be startling when, for example, the starched nurses, stuffy senior physicians, and rumpled interns gathered around a patient's bed in *The Singing Detective* suddenly launch into "Dry Bones"—with all the twists, shakes, and gestures it takes to make the song go. But Potter knew what he was about and had good reasons for what he did.

Potter knew that popular songs, however trivial, can evoke profound emotions. They cannot express the depth of what we feel; it isn't in them to do that; but they have enormous power to recall the feelings we once had. They enable us to recapture the enchantment we knew the first time we heard "our song," for example, even though the song itself may be trite. The old emotion comes bubbling back, but with what Potter calls "a different coating of irony and self knowledge." It is still "our song," even though we are not the same.

How vulnerable we are to melody! The merest fragment of a tune may awaken the deepest nostalgia, all the time telling us that there is no going back. Haven't you found that the silliest songs can turn your heart over even as you try to protect yourself from them by thinking how silly they are?

It is like that not only with the songs Potter used in his plays, but the hymns he remembered from his childhood. As an adult he wanted to laugh at them—they were so simple and sentimental—but he could not, so great was the tug of them. One in particular retained its hold:

> Will there be any stars,
> Any stars in my crown,
> When the evening sun goes down?
> When I wake with the blessed,
> In the mansions of rest,
> Will there be any stars in my crown?

There it is, an evangelical chorus from an English boyhood, wrenching our hearts at the end of *Cold Lazarus*.

Another reason for Potter's peculiar dramatic device is his wish to show that popular culture is an inheritor of something else; that cheap songs, for all their sentimentality, actually do have something of the Psalms of David about them. They are kin to the Psalms when they tell us that the world is other than it is; that there is more to it than meets the eye.

Instances abound. Every time it rains, it rains pennies from heaven. Showers not only threaten to make us wet, but promise to make us rich. When the eyes of our eyes are opened we see that clouds gathered over the hills are really crowds of daffodils. And haven't you discovered that the whole purpose of moonlight is to go with your hair—that it was designed to enhance your evening when you're all dressed up to go dreaming?

The psalmist looks through his eyes in roughly the same way. He gazes at the mountains round about Jerusalem, but what he sees is the Lord round about them that fear Him. That they go

The Fine Art of Being Imperfect

down to the sea in ships, that do business in great waters, see more than waves tossed to and fro by a stormy wind; they behold the works of the Lord and His wonders in the deep:

> Give me a heart to find out Thee,
> And read Thee everywhere.

If this seeing more than meets the eye, this grace of double vision, is the stuff of psalms and songs, it is surely the nerve of poetry, the impulse of music, and the quickening of religion. The poet does not see the world as it is, says Oscar Wilde; if he did, he would cease in that moment to be a poet. Not only so, but the literal eye deceives us. William Blake got it right:

> They ever must believe a lie,
> Who will see *with* not *through* the eye.

Children know how to look at things. In our angel-infancy, eternity shone in the light of common day and something infinite in everything appeared. Don't you remember how hills were higher then? Poets are those who have somehow managed to retain the vision splendid and have kept their sense of wonder, their awareness of something waiting to be revealed or discovered.

Musicians make a similar claim. Ralph Vaughan Williams, that "amiable agnostic," speaks of music as our search for the ultimate, our reaching out to the Eternal, our attempt to reveal something that lies beyond time and appearance.

Some philosophers happily place themselves among the poets and composers. Plato not only believed as they do, but also expressed it unforgettably in his *theory of forms,* which is a poor name for a transcendent idea. He believed that all earthly loveliness is but a faint shadow, a fading reverberation, a falling echo of an infinite and eternal loveliness. Earthly beauty is but a hint, a clue, to what Plotinus called "The Beauty Yonder," so that those who see this world only as it is mistake the image for the reality. Plotinus would say that if the most exquisite musical phrase ever written could be turned into a word, the word would be, not a noun, but an adjective describing a loveliness more lovely still.

You may test all this against your own experience. Don't you remember how one day you read a poem, or looked at a painting, or watched a sunset, or heard a melody that took you in so deep, or carried you out so far, or filled you with such longing that your soul was all but out of you, and you touched the heart of Joy, the Still Point of the turning world?

Psalms and songs that tell us the world is other than it is may be useful in another way; for they may do much more than lead us through sight to insight, from appearance to reality, from facts to meaning. By enabling us to see more than meets the eye they may show us not only a sight for the eyes, but a region of the human Spirit, as well.

William Blake tells us that when he looked at the sun he saw, not a golden circle, the size of a guinea, suspended in the sky; but an innumerable company of angels, clothed in heavenly splendor, praising God and crying Glory! to the Lord of Hosts. A glimpse of the sun not only furnished him with the vocabulary of praise but also quickened his spirit and moved him to adoration.

Not many of us would aspire to Blake's extravagant visions; indeed, we might not even wish for them. But we might well wish for a little more vision than we have. We should have no desire to be counted among the clods, described by Mrs. Browning, who walk on holy ground without knowing it, are unaware that the earth itself is crammed with heaven, and are so intent on plucking blackberries they fail to notice every common bush afire with God. If some have long seen a glory in it all, we should like to catch at least a passing glimpse of it and not be so estranged as to miss the many-splendored thing. Do you remember how Wordsworth described "Peter Bell," a man of this unhappy sort, who never saw more than met his eye?

> A primrose by a river's brim
> A yellow primrose was to him,
> And it was nothing more.

Those who have learned to see through the eye discover flowers of a different sort.

The best and most real daffodils I know are not in Central Park in April, but in Shakespeare eternally. They are the daffodils

> That come before the swallow dares,
> And take the winds of March with beauty.

Autumn is a time of year, but it is no mere season, for Keats has given us a season

> Season of mists and mellow fruitfulness!
> Close bosom-friend of the maturing sun . . .

And that is a season of the soul. The most glorious lark ascends, not from any Irish meadow I ever knew, but in Vaughan Williams' music. That larksong is a rising of the heart, an aspiring of the spirit and then our journey homeward to habitual self.

When dear Joxer Daly, of *Juno and the Paycock* fame, asks his favorite and celebrated and "darlin' " question, "What is the stars? What is the stars?" the answer we give will depend on whether we see *with,* or have learned to see *through*, the eye. Those who see *with* the eye will answer that a star is a huge ball of burning gas; while those who see *through* it will reply, "That is not what a star is, but only what it is made of." Remember Whitman's *Leaves of Grass:*

> When I heard the learn'd astronomer . . . where he lectured with
> much applause in the lecture-room,
> How soon unaccountable I became tired and sick,
> Till rising and gliding out I wander'd off by myself,
> In the mystical moist night-air, and from time to time,
> Looked up in perfect silence at the stars.

The loveliest star I know is the one I talked to as a child when I said,

> Twinkle, twinkle, little star,
> How I wonder what you are!

Such starlight cannot be measured in light-years, for it is a region of the human spirit: a realm of mystery, transcendence and hope.

Seeing through, not with, the eye tells us that the world is not what it is and reveals to us regions of the human spirit. Notice how it may teach us the difference between description and explanation.

Not long ago, an English astrophysicist scolded those scientists, poets, and philosophers who dare to speak of meaning and purpose in the universe. He told them to save their breath to cool their porridge, for talk of that sort is silly. The universe doesn't have any meaning, so we are not going to find it by either heart or head. Life and human intelligence exist by chance. We are not here except by chance, he said.

Now, what is this "chance" that has brought us to life and being? The professor speaks of it as though it were a grand design, an all-encompassing creative energy capable of purposeful action and possessing a mind and intention of its own. Some chance! It is not only my theology that objects to the physicist's view, but my respect for language and the common sense of words. Surely when we speak of chance we mean the very opposite of what he means. We use the word not to explain anything but to confess that we have no explanation. Now, suddenly, we are to believe that chance creates and is responsible for everything.

I think such a way of talking is nonsense. To say that something happened by chance is to say that it happened. The words "by chance" add nothing to our understanding of how and why it happened. They not only fail as explanation, but are useless as description. Chance explains nothing, but rather asks to be explained. Our hope is to get rid of it by discovering what is hiding behind it. Someone said once that chance is a nickname for providence. Our professor goes even further and uses the nickname to deny the providence.

One day during the summer I went walking by the lake. The sun was warm, but not too hot; and the breeze was cool, but not too cold; and I thought to myself what a miracle it was to be so nicely placed in so perfect a temperature. The small wonder suggested a larger one: that the earth seems to be exactly the right distance from the sun. A little closer and we'd perish by fire, a little farther away, by ice. I also found myself wondering how a reductionist of the sort we have considered might reply if I dared tell him my thoughts. I should imagine he would explain that my sense of wonder was misplaced and inappropriate. Had it not occurred to me that if the distance between earth and sun hadn't been right to begin with there could have been no life at all and we shouldn't be around to wonder at the sun on our face? Some explanation! The truth is that the reductionist has said exactly the same thing to me that I said to him. Except that he calls it an explanation, and takes the intellectual high ground, and speaks with the condescension of one who knows, and thinks these poets, philosophers, and musicians an odd lot.

What do I do? I go back to Dennis Potter and the psalmist and *Pennies from Heaven,* and am thankful for those who have kept their sense of wonder in this world of wonders.

4

THE SLANT OF TRUTH

*Do you think there's more than one way
of telling the truth?*

Emily Dickinson wrote a poem in which she exhorts us to "Tell all the truth but tell it slant." That's enough to set the imagination flying off in all directions.

The first quick reaction to it comes, I suppose, from the cynic lurking in each of us, who is glad to hear anything that might seem to support the opinion that all truth is so slanted we should despair of ever finding it. No doubt there is something to be said for the cynic's view, but not much. Of course it would be foolish of us to accept everything we are told at face value. Yet even the cynic believes his cynicism to be true. As someone remarked once, "He who believes in nothing still needs a girl to believe in him."

In any case, cynicism is not what Emily Dickinson is writing about. She exhorts us to tell truth at a slant so as not to be dazzled by it. Straight-on, its brightness may be more than we can bear, for "the truth's superb surprise" threatens to overwhelm us by its power and beauty. Told directly, confronted head-on, truth is sometimes too much for us.

Another poet, Edna St. Vincent Millay, found it so. The glory of an autumn day so ravished her with its gray skies, rolling mists, and colored leaves that she cried out to be delivered from it. Here was passion enough to stretch her apart and snatch the soul out of her, so that, from the pinnacle of ecstasy, she cried out to the

Lord of autumn, "Let fall no burning leaf; prithee, let no bird call."

If some adults can find themselves overwhelmed by "terrible beauty not to be endured," what are we to say of children? The tenderness of childhood is easily hurt by the wound of loveliness. I remember once, when I was a boy, an uncle came to our house and played his violin for us. The music was too much for me. I found it heartbreaking in its poignancy. It seemed that all the tears of the world were in its notes, so that I wept and had to be comforted.

That experience came back to me as I read the biography of Jacqueline du Pré, the superb cellist who died of multiple sclerosis while still a young woman, but whose radiant spirit pervades the recordings she left us.

When she was still a child, Jacqueline's mother brought her to a concert, thinking it a good thing to expose her early to the enchanted world of great music played by accomplished artists. But the little one could not bear it. The sounds of the orchestra were so powerful, and the soloist's playing of Schubert so exquisite, that she drowned out the music with her tears. Never again did her mother take her daughter to hear a soloist play with an orchestra. She resolved that such truth could be told, and such beauty heard, only at a slant, so as gradually to enable her little girl not only to bear, but also to express the loveliness she once had found so overwhelming.

Telling the truth at a slant, then, enables us to grow into it. Head-on, truth may be too much for us; but at a slant we can receive, possess, and grow by it. It takes restraint and patience on someone's part to accomplish this, for as Goethe once complained, "Everybody wants to be somebody: nobody wants to grow."

We must deal gently with our children, then, for they already dwell in a world of beauty difficult to bear. They may not reveal their inconsolable secret, but they know a longing they do not understand and a strangeness of heart that moves, mystifies, and sometimes frightens them. Children cannot speak of the pang of beauty or tell "what wandering voices call from far away"; for, truth to tell, these things are beyond telling.

Our own sadness is that we too quickly lose our childhood's tenderness. We no longer hear those "sweet everlasting voices" and soon forget the heaven that surrounded us in our infancy. The poets speak of it to remind us of all that we knew before we began to forget. As Wordsworth writes,

> There was a time when meadow, grove, and stream,
>> The earth, and every common sight,
>>> To me did seem
>>> Apparelled in celestial light,
>> The glory and the freshness of a dream.
> It is not now as it hath been of yore;—
>> Turn wheresoe'er I may,
>> By night or day,
> The things which I have seen I now can see no more.

"Tell all the truth, but tell it slant," says Emily Dickinson, for its brightness may dazzle. But there are other reasons for the slant of truth. One of them is the manner in which truth comes to us.

Flannery O'Connor speaks of some writers she knew who were eager to claim and boast of "a writer's temperament." She goes on to say that they were not writing much.

O'Connor's own method depended more on discipline than on temperament. She did not waste her time waiting for the right mood or feeling, but sat in front of her typewriter for three hours every morning so that if anything came she would be there to receive it.

There is much to be said for discipline of this sort, which seeks to discover truth head-on; but it is not the only way truth comes to us. It sometimes refuses to be directly engaged, and evades

The Fine Art of Being Imperfect

our frontal assault. It shies away from confrontation and then—having a mind of its own, and a sense of playfulness, and something better to offer us—comes in at a slant, from the margins of the mind, often when we least expect it.

This is another "superb surprise" of truth, and it is ours, not by our striving, but as a gift; not by our effort, but by its own bestowing. Having failed to discover and capture it, we find that it has sought us out and willingly surrendered itself into our hands. I think this is what the newspaper editor meant when he remarked, "In this business, you're working when you're just looking out of the window." Indeed we are, for who knows what may come to mind while we are looking out of a window!

I knew a minister who went into his study every Tuesday morning and wrote his sermon between eight o'clock and noon. His sermons bore all the marks of his method, unfortunately, emerging as great heavy lumps of effortful stuff, with none of the lightsomeness of humor or imagination. He should have spent more time looking out of his window, for imagination takes its own time and requires its own space. Our concentration must always have gaps in it where unexpected meaning may "creep, crawl, flash or thunder in." Our best insights are ours not only by work but by grace; they come to us not only by intensity of thought but as the fruit of passivity.

A. E. Housman used to say that he had to be careful, when shaving, not to allow his mind to "slip into neutral," as it were, for if he did, he could neither anticipate nor control the thoughts that might startle and move him. These thoughts were sometimes hazardous to his health. He describes his experience in the words of Eliphaz the Temanite in the book of Job: "A Spirit passed before my face; the hair of my flesh stood up." When this happened, he was likely to cut himself. It was too high a price to pay for the tingling of truth. High inspiration, no doubt, but blood on the bathroom floor!

Let me share with you one of the finest sentences ever written to describe the creative enterprise. In a letter to her sister, Emily Dickinson wrote, "Art is a house that tries to be haunted." The house cannot be haunted without first being built. That is our task. But having done our work, what we long for is the coming of that Creator Spirit who alone can carry us beyond the level of our craft, elevate our achievement above mere self-expression, and infuse it with a greater than individual significance. As Hemingway put it, "Most of the time I write as well as I can; occasionally I write better."

You have discovered this for yourself, for you know that, whatever the nature of your work, the best you have accomplished has not come from you but through you: "Not I, not I, but the wind that blows through me," cried D. H. Lawrence; and anyone who is more than a mere doodler with the tools of his trade knows what Lawrence meant.

Thelonious Monk, who composed some of the greatest jazz ever written, would have understood Lawrence perfectly. Monk would wander for days in the streets of Manhattan: south as far as Sixtieth, north as far as Seventieth, west as far as the river; and three blocks east of there. He walked all wrapped up in himself, figuring out his music, dwelling in his own world of themes and variations before returning home to his dear Nellie to write the music he had sought, and which had found him, on his travels.

It ought not to surprise us, then, to read that Moses saw God going but not coming; that he could not gaze upon the face of his Creator, but managed to catch a passing glimpse of His back. The Divine Word reached him at a slant, else how could he hear it or, hearing it, bear it? We should not wonder that God hid His face from Elijah, or that the mountain-dwelling prophet heard himself addressed, not in the earthquake, fire and wind, but in "a sound of gentle stillness."

Note, finally, that truth should be told at a slant because truth is safe only when it is spoken in love.

The Fine Art of Being Imperfect

Most of us have suffered at one time or other from the sort of person who boasts that he "tells the truth regardless" and is proud of his honesty and courage. But those to whom he speaks the truth regardless are less likely to be impressed by his courage than appalled at his insensitivity. If it is true that love without truth is sometimes sentimental, it must also be acknowledged that truth without love can be terribly cruel, for "human kind cannot bear very much reality." Notice the kindness of the restraint of Jesus when on one occasion He said to His disciples, "I have many things to tell you, but you could not bear them now." Paul catches His spirit perfectly when he tells us quite simply that "love knows when to be silent."

I knew a man who had been unfaithful to his wife. It happened once, and the man immediately regretted and repented of his faithlessness. His sense of shame was deep and genuine, and the thought of what he had done remained abhorrent to him. But one evening he tried to ease his guilt by telling his wife what he had done, and by his confession laid a heavy weight of suffering on her. There can be no doubt that it was honest of him to do so, but it was his wife, and not he, who bore the cost of his honesty. He should have remembered that "love knows when to be silent" and should not have sought to ease his conscience by inflicting such anguish on her. Perhaps part of the price of his unfaithfulness was that he should suffer it alone.

Think of those thoughtless ones who call up family or friends and tell them bad news late at night. Those who receive the news are often unable to do anything about it before morning, and would be better able to cope with it after a good night's sleep. So why tell them? Spare them the unhappy knowledge; allow them their rest, and tell them in the morning.

Physicians are now spending more time learning to tell the truth kindly. They have not always done so. They have sometimes been guilty of what one physician calls "terminal candor" in sharing grave news with their patients: a candor recently described in *The New York Times* as "the rape of hope." Young physicians are now learning to balance their patients' need to know with a concern for the patient's spirit.

What we are saying in all this is that the truth we know is not something separate from the rest of our nature and all the other qualities we possess. If it is, then it quickly ceases to be true and may even become demonic. As Blake warned us,

> A truth that's told with bad intent
> Beats all the lies you can invent.

Why should the truth we see be divorced from our wisdom, sensitivity, and kindness, as though it were a bit of stuff with an independent life of its own, having no connection with our experience or character? Truth is part of our person. It is safe only when it is the twin of kindness and the friend of love. Those who seek it must find not only honesty, but grace; not only candor, but mercy. The heart can celebrate truth only when it has learned to rejoice in love.

The Fine Art of Being Imperfect

5

FALSE GODS
AND THE DEVIL TO PAY

Is it always a good thing to believe in God?

Most of us assume that it is a good thing to believe in God; that it is somehow better to be a believer, any kind of believer, than to be an atheist or even an agnostic. I'm not so sure. I think it all depends on the kind of God we believe in.

When Jacqueline du Pré, that superb cellist, fell madly in love and married the man she adored, she surrendered her nominal Christianity to embrace the faith of her husband, who was Jewish. A few years later, the first signs of the multiple sclerosis that was to end her career, and then her life, appeared. She bore her illness with grace and fortitude; but one of the hardest things she had to put up with was that two of the people closest to her—one of them her fundamentalist Christian mother—told her that God had afflicted her with MS because she had surrendered her faith. Is it a good thing to believe in a God like that?

William Barclay was a Scottish biblical scholar whose writings have been enormously helpful to both ministers and laity for over sixty years. One bright summer afternoon, while on holiday in Ireland, his daughter and son-in-law went sailing, only to perish in a sudden squall. Soon after, Professor Barclay received an anonymous letter telling him that God had drowned his dear ones to get even with him for his heretical teaching. The letter, being anonymous, was unanswerable; but Barclay said that if he could have answered the writer it would have been in the words of John Wesley: "Your God is my devil!" Is it a good thing to believe in a God like that?

Does the psalmist believe in a God of that sort when he warns us, "Their sorrows shall be multiplied who run after another God?" It sounds so much like a threat that it would be easy to make his words into what George MacDonald called a "mean theology," and suppose that the God of the psalmist is jealous and vicious, out to damage those who no longer wish to honor Him. He sounds like a jilted lover who in bitterness resolves, "If I can't have her, no one else will."

The psalmist means nothing of the sort. His warning against other gods does not arise from the pettiness of the God he worships, but is quickened by the Divine splendor. God is that Gracious Personal Reality greater than whom nothing can be conceived; the fountain of all goodness; the perfection of wisdom, love, and power, whose imperishable breath is in our nostrils and whose tender mercies are over all His works. The psalmist is bewildered that anyone would wish to turn from Him, for He has no equal. To forsake His worship and run after another God is to pursue a lesser god. It is to repudiate the Highest to embrace the trivial.

To worship means to ascribe worth. To worship anything less than the highest we know is to ascribe worth to what we know is not worthy; it is to value what is not valuable; to praise what does not deserve to be praised; to honor what ought not to be honored and to approve what is not excellent. It is to give a standing ovation to a trivial work, indifferently performed, by an undistinguished artist. It is to be diminished by choice. Yet we do it all the time.

At the end of his life Malcolm Muggeridge confessed that what bothered him most was not any sin either of commission or omission, nothing done or left undone to be repented of; but that he had picked the third-rate over the first-rate and had gone after

The Fine Art of Being Imperfect

the worst when he could have had the best. He had chosen cardboard shoes when he might have had leather; processed cheese when he could have had cheddar; artificial flowers when the primroses were out.

Surely the psalmist is both wise and kind to warn us that our sorrows will be multiplied by that kind of perverseness. And if our sorrows are multiplied, it is not because God is mean but because life is moral. If we revere the tenth-rate we cannot expect to be first-rate. If we honor what is inferior we shall soon lose our ability to recognize, our capacity to appreciate, and our desire to possess what is excellent.

And that is why God is jealous. He is not jealous *of* us, for there is no good thing He would not wish us to have; but He is jealous *for* us, desiring that we should have *only* what is good. Loving parents are like that. When they see the children of their heart pursuing ends that are not worthy of them, they are grieved and will do all they can to show them a better way. For love is inexorable; indeed, only love is inexorable. It refuses either to let us off or give us up until we have learned to cherish what is good.

One reason for this loving vigilance is that ultimately we become like the gods we worship. What we choose is what we are, and what we love we yet shall be.

No one saw this more clearly than Dante, who declared in every part of his work that we are punished, not so much for our sins, as by them; for they fashion us in their own image. We assume their nature. We begin even to look like them. In Dante's underworld every punishment fits the crime, for every figure portrays its own transgression.

This is true not only in Dante's world. If we lie we become false, for we cannot keep our lie outside us. If we give ourselves to sensuality we soon are unable to think of anything else. If we worship money we become misers "with eyes like little dollars in the dark." And if we worship a cruel god, we shall not only do his work but also carry his likeness on our soul.

False Gods and the Devil to Pay

But there is more: Hastening after another god will not only spoil our image, it will wound our humanity, for the god we are most likely to catch up with is ourselves. Hamlet says:

> What a piece of work is a man, how noble in reason, how infinite in faculties, in form and moving how express and admirable, in action how like an angel in apprehension how like a god. . . .

Being so much like a god can easily go to our heads and make it a short step to self-worship. For we cannot worship what we know is beneath us, and we have left nothing above us. God has made us in His likeness, and if we cease to worship the Creator, what is left but to adore the created image? This is Eden's temptation and the original sin: "You shall be as gods." Swinburne put it plainly in his *Hymn of Man:*

> Glory to Man in the highest!
> For Man is the Master of things.

Now, the trouble with all this is that when we snatch at equality with God we don't act like God, but begin to act like the devil. It is not that pride goes before a fall, but that our pride is our fall. Our overreaching leads to all kinds of mischief.

The events of our time demonstrate this. A distinguished theologian once proposed that Adolf Hitler be awarded an honorary Doctor of Divinity degree from a good university, posthumously, thank God, for demonstrating better than any theologian ever had the sorrows that multiply when we think we are God.

Hitler said we should look to heaven to see clouds and birds, but for no other reason. He meant that heaven is for the birds, for there is no god higher than our own heads. There is nothing above us to which we owe allegiance or from which we might draw help. We must choose our values without reference to any being

38   *The Fine Art of Being Imperfect*

other than the human being, and we are perfectly capable of so choosing them.

So Hitler set himself up as his own god and became a monster. The master of the master race, who thought himself capable of determining human values, quickly determined that some races have no value except for the rings on their fingers and the gold fillings in their teeth. The first casualty of his sort of humanism was our humanity.

The author of the book of Daniel saw this clearly and declared it unforgettably. When King Nebuchadnezzar of Babylon forgot that the heavens rule and puffed himself up with the glory of his city and made himself the god of his empire, he found himself banished from the company of men and put out to grass with the animals. Refusing to look to heaven, he found himself in the company of beasts, chewing the cud and licking the earth.

We learn from Daniel that we are unstable creatures, wobbling between God and the animals, managing to keep our human image only by wearing the image of the Divine. That likeness repudiated, we sink to the level of beasts, and because we are such clever animals, to depths of bestiality no animal ever conceived.

Belshazzar succeeded Nebuchadnezzar but learned nothing from his father's warning. He did the same bad things over again, only worse. Daniel tells us that Belshazzar was "weighed in the balance and found wanting," which is a way of saying he was a lightweight—a two-bit monarch who believed the flatterers who told him he was a King of Kings and would live forever.

Hastening after other gods will spoil our image and wound our humanity; it will also multiply our sorrows by prostituting our religion.

It has often been pointed out how thoroughly the most demonic "isms" of our time assumed the likeness of religion. Both the revived paganism of the Nazis and the atheistic materialism of the Communists boasted of their saints, prophets, relics, heroes, and martyrs. They asserted their sense of destiny and on their holy days ritualized it with incense, symbols, scripture, and sacred songs and solos. They had their own catechisms, Mao's "Little Red Book" among them. They even killed their heretics and persecuted their reformers.

Just the other day, I saw a cartoon called "The Communist Sunday School," by Max Beerbohm. On the walls were pictures of "Attractive Trotsky" and "Lively Lenin," while the incomparable Max described the goings-on as "Pupils learning that they must not shrink from shedding blood in order to achieve starvation."

Paul Tillich called these "isms" pseudoreligions, while Karl Barth, who set himself and his own faith against them in Hitler's Germany, described them as "disguised religions." Whatever they were called, and however disguised, nothing in history has matched their evil or rivaled their barbarism. They make the psalmist's words "Their sorrows shall be multiplied that hasten after another God" the text of the century, for they are a commentary on this century's events and tragedy. Its "sorrows multiplied" included two World Wars and other wars besides, the Holocaust, and the Gulag. One hundred and fifty million people have been killed by state violence in our time. Six million Jews were slaughtered by Hitler and twenty million Russians by Stalin. One third of the population of Kampuchea was massacred, while the extent of Mao's atrocities is not yet known or added up.

Fifty years ago, William Temple, Archbishop of Canterbury, said that the world would be saved by worship, and went on to tell us what he meant by it. He said that to worship is to feed the mind with the truth of God, to purge the imagination with the beauty of God, to quicken the conscience with the holiness of God, to open the heart to the love of God, to devote the will to the purpose of God.

The Fine Art of Being Imperfect

That didn't seem much to set against the passionate intensity of dictators and totalitarian regimes; yet it is an enduring conviction that has outlasted them. For you and I live in the age of the death of humanism. As historian Paul Johnson tells us, it "lingers on only in the home of lost causes." The "other gods," so ardently pursued and so confidently hastened-after, are gods that failed. They were consumed in the conflagration they kindled on the earth. We have lived through their twilight. We now dwell in the promise that while sorrow may tarry for the night, joy comes with the morning.

6

THE FINE ART
OF BEING IMPERFECT

Do you find it harder to be perfect or to be imperfect?

When I asked several of my friends if they found it harder to be perfect or to be imperfect, they couldn't wait to tell me how hard they found it to be imperfect—that is, to live with their imperfections. They know that to be perfect is impossible; yet the very idea of perfection makes it hard for them to be reconciled to their limitations. So they become part of that company of tormented and tormenting souls who know they can't be perfect, but can't bear to be anything less.

"Tormented" describes them well, for they are hard on themselves. No matter how good they are they never think they're good enough. However much they accomplish, they succeed only in disappointing their own high expectations. When the only success they will acknowledge is perfection, anything less must be counted failure. So they have come to interpret themselves by a cluster of unhappy words: inferiority, guilt, anxiety, quiet desperation—sometimes even self-contempt and despair.

This struggle against our sense of inferiority and failure is unrelenting. At times we think we've overcome it; favorable circumstances and worthy accomplishments strengthen our confidence for a little while. But then some new threat to our self-esteem awakens all the accusing voices we hoped had been silenced. Now they are louder, more insistent—indeed more

from a pure and perfect motive. If one whiff of self-interest is detected, their whole enterprise, however worthy, is abandoned. Their desire for perfection therefore paralyzes them, for no motive is ever entirely pure. Yet it never occurs to them that their moral elitism may be self-serving, or that a needy world cries out even for their imperfect help.

Before we embark on any enterprise we ought to ask ourselves if it is worth doing and if we can do it. If it is, and we can, then we should get on with it, however mixed our motives.

All of this reminds me of G. K. Chesterton, who mocks our pretensions by announcing that if a thing is worth doing, it is worth doing badly. He saves us from despair in an astonishing way—by making a high use of the doctrine of original sin. He calls it "the only cheerful doctrine," for it tells us that nothing is as it should be; that imperfection is neither peculiar to us, nor incidental to our world, but fundamental to any understanding of ourselves and our world. It is not merely that we disappoint others; we ourselves are vulnerable and may be disappointed by them and suffer from their carelessness.

Chesterton has a word for those of us who think we must always be at our best. He tells us that if all we can offer is our best, we are not offering enough, for our best is only a very small part of us. If I were to offer my congregation only my best, I think I'd preach about one Sunday in seven—*they* might say one in ten. What should I do on the days when I'm not at my best? Should I not show up? I can't afford to wait for a pure heart, a perfect motive, and to be always at my best before doing anything; for life is short, and these things are already late in coming.

Our failures are no surprise to God, for He never expected us to be perfect. We really mustn't think that God is foolish enough to be astonished by imperfections that are no surprise even to us, or that He is estranged from us because of them. We are not accepted by God because we are perfectly acceptable; we are accepted because we are perfectly loved.

The Fine Art of Being Imperfect

45

I heard of a woman who thought herself so dreadfully wicked she doubted whether God could forgive her. But when she mentioned it to Him, He replied, "Don't be silly! I had a far more difficult case than yours just yesterday."

> Once in a saintly passion
> I cried with desperate grief
> Ah! Lord, my heart is full of guile,
> Of sinners I am chief.
> Then stooped my guardian angel
> And whispered from behind,
> "Vanity! my little man,
> You're nothing of the kind."

Let me close by telling you of another sort of pottery—rougher, tougher, and older even than Belleek. The prophet Jeremiah saw it when he visited the house of the potter and watched him as he wrought a work at his wheel. The vessel he made of clay was marred in the hands of the potter, so he made it into another vessel, as seemed good to the potter to make it. The imperfect article was not discarded, but reshaped, reformed by those strong hands and skillful fingers until it pleased the potter's eye and satisfied his heart. When it was finished, it was, like all works of art, not perfect, but unique, beautiful, and useful.

Jeremiah's experience was not merely an incident, but a parable. It taught the prophet that God does not have one perfect plan for us that, once disappointed, condemns us to languish in vain regret forever. For God is like the potter. His hands are always on us, making us over again, again, and again, until we satisfy His heart's desire and our own heart's dream.

On a recent Sunday afternoon, I looked for a cab on Central Park West, but the only one I could find was going south, and I wanted to go north. I jumped in anyway, and the driver made a sweeping U-turn, and pulled up behind a police cruiser parked at a traffic light. I thought the cabby was in trouble, and said so. "Not a bit of it," he told me. "U-turns are permitted in New York City." I really didn't believe him and asked a traffic-cop about it a day later. My cab driver was right. U-turns are permitted in New York City except on those streets where signs expressly forbid them.

U-turns are allowed. You don't need to worry about being perfect—that is, about being imperfect—once you discover how delightful it can be to turn yourself around.

7

WAYS OF LOVING

How do you treat people you don't like?

For religious faith, the highest virtue is love—not unselfishness! Love is not merely a denial of the self, for the sake of the self, but a positive care for the well-being of others and an active seeking of their good.

The reason for this is that God is love, so that to love is to share the Divine nature. As the Scriptures say, "The unloving know nothing of love." The two greatest commandments of Christianity are that we should love God with our whole heart, and our neighbors as ourselves.

Yet the word *love* is used to describe so many feelings of the heart, convictions of the mind, determinations of the will, and actions of the body, in such a variety of relations, that it is sometimes hard to know what we mean when we speak of it. Indeed, Reinhold Niebuhr once warned that we are never more dangerous than when we act from love, because love can lull the conscience to sleep and hide from us our insensitivity and selfishness. Believing that love is enough, we may neglect the claims of courtesy and respect, forgetting that love is safe only when it is just and wise.

Shakespeare knew this well and made two of his greatest tragic heroes say so. Othello sets it down that he is one "who loved not wisely, but too well," and Lear knows himself to be "a foolish, fond old man." Yet our fondness does not excuse our foolishness, nor does it save us from its consequences. Indeed, it may make us unaware that we love others for our own sake as well as theirs, that our care for them is tinged with self-interest, and that seeking their good may be a way of realizing our own.

So here are four exhortations, little more than elaborate adjectives, to heighten our awareness and make our love more loving.

1. Our affection should be considerate.

I know a mother who is sure that her love for her children excuses her inexcusable prying into their personal affairs. She thinks that her affection gives her the right to intrude. She also knows that her children's love for her makes it hard for them to oppose her. As a result, her children feel guilty if they resist her and resentful if they don't.

C. S. Lewis tells of having lunch with a minister and the minister's wife, and their two children, home from university for the weekend. The minister's children were intelligent, informed, and interesting, yet all through the meal the father dismissed their opinions with an impatience that bordered on rudeness. There was no doubt of his care for them, yet his affection was disrespectful. He was both loving and insensitive, both caring and careless.

At the same time, the children's affection for their parents made them reluctant to risk a confrontation with their father which they knew would be upsetting to their mother. So they picked at their food until they could decently make their escape.

We sometimes say that because home is a place of genuine affection we can be more natural there, more free to speak our minds and be ourselves, knowing that we shall be heard, understood, and accepted. Such talk is often sentimental nonsense. For many, home is the one place where they do not feel free to say what they think or express what they feel.

Children can be every bit as inconsiderate as their parents, carelessly and sometimes arrogantly dismissing what their parents have to say because they *are* their parents. Familiarity, if it does not always breed contempt, is a frequent cause of estrangement when we fail to see that our affection demands a particular degree of courtesy and good manners.

Our affection should be considerate.

2. Our friendship should be disinterested.

Richard Ingrams wrote a book about the lifelong friendship of three men, Hesketh Pearson, Hugh Kingsmill, and Malcolm Muggeridge. He called it *God's Apology,* from a saying of Hugh Kingsmill that "Friends are God's apology for relations."

Muggeridge loved to say that the most valued quality of friendship is that it is disinterested. He did not mean by this that friends are not interested in one another—of course they are— but that they are disinterested; that is, they are not in the relationship for anything other than friendship. Their friends are not means to some other end, but are ends in themselves. They are not to be used, but to be enjoyed.

Indeed, friends are not friends even for friendship. You must have noticed that people who are always looking for friends seldom find any. We don't discover friends by wanting them, but by wanting something else. We picture lovers face to face, but friends seldom look at each other; their eyes are elsewhere, discovering truth, exploring beauty, scrutinizing faith, examining opinions. My friends are always looking at charts, or gazing out to sea. They read poems and listen to music and love to talk about what they read and hear and think. Our answers do not always agree, but we agree about the questions that are worth asking. And we care for and trust each other.

These conditions of friendship are few and simple, and there is little about them that would keep others out. Of lovers we say, "Two's company, three's a crowd." But new friends are welcome, each winning a unique response from each to the enrichment of all. Being kindred spirits, they end our loneliness without spoiling our solitude, and bring the gifts of ease and quiet.

The Fine Art of Being Imperfect

Maxim Gorky one day came upon Tolstoy sitting on a rock by the ocean, looking out to sea, and wrote that he would not be an orphan on the earth so long as Tolstoy lived on it.

Keep your affection considerate and your friendship disinterested.

3. We should make our passion personal.

We used to speak of making love; now we talk of having sex. But they are not the same, and it is not the puritan in me, but the romantic in me that wishes to preserve the difference and deplores the way the wind is blowing.

You can discover what I mean by comparing two movies, one old and the other new. Who, having seen the film, could ever forget Deborah Kerr and Cary Grant in *An Affair to Remember?* And who, having seen it, would wish to remember Annette Benning and Warren Beatty in *Love Affair,* its recent remake? The earlier lovers were so full of grace and wit and restraint and charm and cherishing that they broke our hearts. And the more recent ones are so empty of these qualities that we really don't care what happens to them.

Having sex may be simply one more way of indulging our selfishness. Somebody said once that when a young man whispers, "I love you," he sometimes means, "I love me, and I want you." And that means it isn't love he feels, it's sex he's after.

And what is sex but a function we share with the animals? As Cole Porter and Eartha Kitt tell us eloquently, "Birds do it, bees do it . . . even cold New England clams do it." Sex is part of our animal nature, entrusted to us so that we can make it human. We won't humanize it by behaving like the animals.

I am astonished by those who think that our sharing an animal function means that we are being natural when we act like beasts. Surely we act naturally when we behave humanly by refusing to allow our animal appetites to get ahead of our human qualities of friendship, responsibility, restraint, devotion, and faithfulness. In other words, we act naturally by making our passion personal.

To have sex, any woman or man will suffice; but to make love, only this man or woman. When we make love, what we desire is not a body, *any* body; but this person, so dear and so cherished, with every quality and feature so infinitely precious that no one else will do. And if you think that this will spoil your pleasure or diminish your delight, then you have forgotten that most of this world's great love poetry was written by men and women who believed what I have just described.

To find such a love is the death of winter; it is springtime, Maytime; it is soft breezes and fragrant airs in woods and meadows; it is birdsong at dawn and gentle light at evening.

Let your affection be considerate, your friendship disinterested, and your passion personal.

4. Our charity should be kind.

Sometimes it isn't. It may be cold and condescending. Indeed, our charity can be humiliating when it is lacking in humility—when it does not recognize that giving is a kind of receiving and that those who take from us are, in the very same act, giving to us.

This kindness of our charity solves another problem. The difficulty many have with the commandment to love our neighbors is that our neighbors may not be lovable, and love cannot be commanded. Our love is not under the control of our will. If it were, most of the great love stories would never have been written, including *Tristan and Isolde, Eloise and Abelard, Romeo and Juliet*.

That is why so many good people feel discouraged, believing that when they are commanded to love their neighbors they are required to like everybody. They know that they don't, and that they can't, and that they may not even wish to.

The Fine Art of Being Imperfect

Michael Kinsley wrote in *The New Yorker* of a woman who manages to like everybody "by always making the crucial, if puzzling, distinction between the individual and everything he or she stands for." Now this may be easy if you don't have much character of your own, but I shouldn't wish to be capable of it.

It is here that Samuel Johnson comes to our rescue with one of the most liberating sentences he ever wrote: "Kindness is in our power, fondness is not." Charity is a love that can be commanded because kindness is within our power. It is not felt, but willed. Charity is not passion or affection or friendship, but an attitude of unshakable and unwearied goodwill to others, whether we like them or not. I could give you a list as long as my arm of people I don't like; but I love every one of them by the goodwill I bear them, and I could not be unkind to them.

If that sounds difficult, then we should remember it is exactly how we love ourselves. I don't always like myself, but I always love myself by having a deep and unshakable concern for my well-being, and I hold myself in unwearied goodwill. To love our neighbors as ourselves is to extend the same courtesy to others.

And then, sometimes, a miracle happens. The action that is willed becomes an affection that is felt. The kindness that began as obedience to a command becomes a fondness that is an impulse of our heart. We have not only thought ourselves into a new way of acting; we have acted ourselves into a new way of feeling.

Affection, friendship, kindness, and passion are ways of loving that we have separated to aid our thinking and help our understanding. Yet sometimes they become gloriously confused or, rather, wonderfully blended into a single, simple, joyous awareness, and we know ourselves kin to Him whose love is shed abroad in our hearts by His loving Spirit.

Such moments are sublime and transcendent. They reach beyond time to become "the Still Point of our turning world." In them we know ourselves touched by that love which moves the sun and all the other stars.

8

DREAMS WITHIN
A DREAM

Do you think God understands radar?

The words, "I believe in God, the Father Almighty, Maker of heaven and earth," begin a Christian creed, but it was the faith of Israel that first thought of them. They have grown a little stale since then, surpassed or usurped by fresh explanations of the beginning of things, which, if they have not exactly eliminated God from the universe, have moved Him to the margins of our thought concerning it. "The Father Almighty" has become "The Grandfather Unnecessary," who is both literally and figuratively "long ago and far away." Outdated and out-distanced, He is really nowhere. "The Ancient of Days" is not the kind of description we like to see on a résumé nowadays, not even God's.

J. B. Phillips, who was among the first to translate the Christian Scriptures into modern English, once asked a group of university students if they thought God understood radar. They thought He did not. That sly old fox, Robert Frost, did something similar with a group of young men and women who had assembled in a famous New England college to hear him read his poetry. "Does the universe have a purpose?" he asked. They thought it didn't. "Are you capable of having purposes?" was his next question. They said they were. The poet then asked, "Do you think that the purpose of the universe might be that you should have purposes?"

Now, that's a good question. It is not that purposes in a purposeless universe have no point to them; they have too much point to them! It is not that minds in a mindless world do not make sense; they make too much sense! It is hard to believe that minds were created mindlessly or that our ability to act purposefully was brought about accidentally. To believe that is like saying that while Lady Macbeth was capable of acting with cunning deliberation and crafty intent, the play *Macbeth* itself was written by a chimpanzee.

How can we everywhere discover minds that are made, including our own, and deny the mind of the Maker? How can we experience a rational world and consider its origin irrational; or believe that the universe, which seems more and more like a great thought, is the result of two blind children, Chance and Accident, making mud pies in the dark? Frost couldn't make that add up, and he wrote an amusing poem about it, called "Accidentally on Purpose."

While watching *The Discovery Channel,* I discovered that there was a time in the history of dinosaurs when they began to change rapidly. They grew bigger, for one thing, and their basic nature was exaggerated. The aggressive ones became more aggressive and the defensive ones more defensive. The vegetarians ate more vegetables, and the carnivores ate more vegetarians. One of the defensive ones went so far as to grow a club at the end of its tail with which it proceeded to bash anything that looked at it with bad intent.

Now, who thought of a tail like that? Did the dinosaur? And if it did, was the power of positive thinking powerful enough to ensure its growth? Does dinosaur wishing really make it so? The explanation mentioned in passing was that the tail "evolved," which means, I suppose, that some genetic mechanism passed the word that a club was needed, and what was needed was provided.

The "explanation" may be true. Indeed, I am inclined to think it true, except that it is not an explanation. It just changes the question and adds to its complexity. Now I hardly care where the club came from; what really interests me is where the hereditary mechanism that produced it came from! How did it know to establish and preserve those functions most necessary to survival? Did someone tell it how to do so? Or if, as we are sometimes told, everything was accomplished by "natural selection," how did the selection find its "nature"?

We may say that things simply evolved like that, but "simply evolved" is not as simple as it sounds. Why did they evolve like that? No doubt, everything has a mechanism of some sort by which it works, for everything must work in some way. Nothing works in no way. But how are we to account for the mechanism? How does it know to work in the way it works? Is there, as the poet believes, a Presence, a Mind "too instant to be known" perfectly hidden in creation, in the words of Moffit,

> The silent mover of the play,
> The focus of its myriad parts.

The Creator Spirit may have moved silently, but those who beheld His work did not. How could they when they considered the wonders of His fashioning! He laid the foundation of the earth and wrapped it in a garment of cloud; He opened the springs of the sea, and commanded its proud waves, and scattered the east wind, and made a way for the lightning of the thunder; He shaped the treasures of the snow, and by Him the drops of dew were formed; He caused the dayspring to know its place, and declared the region where light dwells, and imparted the sweet influences of Pleiades and Orion. No wonder that on the first day of the world the morning stars sang together, and all the sons of God shouted for joy, and the children of the dawn danced their praise!

The Fine Art of Being Imperfect

John Moffit's phrase, "the silent mover of the play," gives us another reason to place Mind or Spirit at the center of our thought of creation. It suggests that God makes the world as novelists make characters or dramatists make *dramatis personae.* Such creation is neither remote for the Creator nor passive for the created.

Richard Strauss and Hugo von Hofmannsthal discovered this when their opera *Der Rosenkavalier* resisted all their efforts to make it what they had intended it to be. The composer and librettist had thought to write "a thoroughly comic opera, as bright and obvious as a pantomime," but it did not turn out that way. When they got into their work, the Marschallin, who in their original intent had no claim to either distinction or preeminence, captured their imagination and took them over. She inspired their best lines and their most sublime music in such a way as to reshape her own character and transform the nature of the work. The opera was now closer to tragedy than to comedy, more dark than bright, more profound than lightsome.

If that is how the Maker of heaven and earth creates, then He must be at it all the time! His supreme skill is not in merely making things but in allowing things to make themselves. This means that He enables us to be truly ourselves, expressing our own will, displaying our own character, acting from the inner consistency and necessity of our own nature. Yet at all times and in every moment He so encloses our action within His own as to give our character a formative part in His drama. The Prince of Denmark is both his own man and Shakespeare's Hamlet. The Marschallin belongs both to herself and to Richard Strauss. Paul put it perfectly for all who know the Creator Spirit: "I . . . yet not I, but the grace of God."

We have thought of the Maker of heaven and earth as the Mind of the world and as the supreme Dramatist or Composer. Jeremiah had another image, for he visited the house of the potter and watched him as he wrought a work at his wheel.

The vessel the potter made of clay was marred in his hands, so he made it into another vessel as seemed good to the potter to make it. The imperfect article was not discarded, but reshaped, reformed by those strong hands and skillful fingers, until what they held pleased the potter's eye and satisfied his heart. When it was finished it was, like all works of art, not perfect, but unique, beautiful, and useful.

Jeremiah's experience was not merely an incident, but a parable. It taught the prophet that God does not have one perfect plan for us that, once disappointed, condemns us to languish in vain regret. God is like the potter whose hands are always on us, making us over again, again, and again, until we satisfy His heart's desire and our own heart's dream. And creation as a dream is the loveliest image of all.

It is thoroughly biblical, as you will recognize at once by remembering Joseph, the "beautiful dreamer" of Israel's history and your own childhood. His story is inseparable from dreams: not only his own, for which his brothers hated him and sold him into slavery in Egypt; but also Pharaoh's dreams and those of his butcher and baker and candlestick maker, which Joseph wisely interpreted, thereby rising to power as Pharaoh's favorite.

"Things come 'round," as we say, and when they do, here are Joseph's brethren, terrified that their brother, on whom their lives now depend, will bear a grudge against them for the evil they have done. But not a bit of it; for Joseph believes that what they meant for evil, God intended for good. They had not sent him to Egypt; God had brought him there to accomplish His own purpose and fulfill His own loving intention. All of which is Joseph's way of saying that the "Beautiful Dreamer" of his own story is not Joseph, but God. His own dreams, and Pharaoh's too, are but dreams within a Dream.

This meant that when Joseph's dreams became a nightmare of envy, hatred, treachery, seduction, and disgrace, the real Dream did not fail or falter, but redeemed the time by gathering even the evil of his days into an all-encompassing goodness.

On one of the Hebridean Islands there lived a woman lovely of face, gentle of speech, graceful in form and bearing, and so elegant in spirit and splendid of mind it was said she might have wedded a king. Instead, she married a shy man, quiet and slow of speech, who loved the companionship of the hills. Only once did she give answer to those who wondered at her choice, and that was when she said, "I sold my dreams for love, and found love better than all my dreams."

9
ALL THAT JAZZ

Does the song you came to sing remain unsung?

Geoff Dyer has written a book about jazz and called it, *But Beautiful* (New York: Farrar, Straus and Giroux, 1991). It is worth twenty dollars of anybody's money—not only for what it has to tell us about jazz, but for what jazz has to tell us about life.

Near the start, we meet a plump German tourist who spotted Billie Holiday and Lester Young one evening when Lady and Pres were waiting for a cab. The conversation went something like this:

> "You are one of the two greatest singers of this century," the tourist told her.
>
> "Who's the other?" Lady asked.
>
> "Maria Callas," he replied. "It is a tragedy you have not sung together."
>
> Then, turning to her companion, he continued, "And you must be the great Lester Young, The President, the man who learned to whisper on the tenor when everyone wanted to shout."
>
> He beamed on them, asked for their autographs, wrote his address on an envelope, and invited them to visit him in Hamburg.

What the tourist said about Pres was true; only he made Young's accomplishments seem effortless when it had not been easy for him to find his voice. Too many people had expected him to shout—had wanted him to play like Coleman Hawkins, who had defined how the tenor sax should be played, by blowing hard for a big sound. Young's voice was more restrained, held back, with only a hint and a promise of breaking loose. He made not only his music, but also his instrument, a lightsome thing; for he breathed a gentler air, tender and touching in its wistfulness. It took a while for those accustomed to a more robust sound to recognize that Young's was not inferior and wrong, but different and right.

It was strangely fitting that the tourist should mention Maria Callas in his snatch of conversation with Lady and Pres, for Callas was not only a great singer, as Billie Holiday was, she sang the way Young played. Will Crutchfield, one of our most astute music critics, in an article in *The New Yorker,* said that Callas's distinctive contribution to opera was that she had the courage to sing softly. His comment reminded me of Isobel Baillie, an English soprano of an earlier generation of singers, who called her autobiography, *Never Sing Louder Than Lovely.*

How does one find one's voice and the courage to sing softly if that is what it calls for? Oddly enough, by imitation: by listening to the great, by learning from them, and even by trying to be like them. If we have any quality of our own, and if we have anything to say, we shall soon wish to express ourselves in our own voice and with our own sound. We need not think that we are better—only that we are different, and that we must succeed or fail in our own distinctive way.

When I was fourteen years old and had discovered that I loved to preach and was likely, if I had my way, to spend the rest of my life doing it, I listened to every preacher within an unreasonable distance. There were lots of them, and they came in all varieties. Some were loud and some soft; some were dramatic and others conversational in style; some made me cringe, and others left me tingling: but good, bad, or indifferent, they were all grist for my mill.

So were the great actors, and the writers and readers of poetry. How different they were from one another, from the sly mumbling of Robert Frost and the vagueness of Yeats, to Dylan Thomas, who read better than any of them, and sang, not only in his chains, but in his speech, and lilted the music of his own rhyming and the rhythms of every poet he loved.

I had my heroes, of course; and I imitated those I most admired. I borrowed a gesture here, an inflection there. I even wished for a Scottish accent instead of an Irish one, but only for a short time. As the formative years passed, I began to discover my own truth and express it in my own voice. When I think of those who influenced me, I know I am not like any of them; but I remain enormously indebted to all of them.

There is a sort of imitation that does not enable us to find our voice but ensures that we shall never find it. Successful imitators discover that their success is their punishment; for they have made themselves copies of the genuine article, the real thing. Witness the hundreds of would-be Elvises, each of them the spitting image of his idol in everything except originality and talent. They are like the baseball autographs that are sold complete with a certificate of authenticity proving them genuine reproductions. If we are really good at imitation, we may become more like those we imitate than they are. Charlie Chaplin once entered a Chaplin look-alike contest and came in seventh.

Imitation of this sort means a loss of self. I am haunted by the sad and beautiful words of Rabindranath Tagore, "The song I came to sing remains unsung: I have spent my days stringing and unstringing my instrument." Nathaniel Hawthorne once made notes in his diary for "a story in which the chief character never appears." At three o'clock in the morning, which someone has called "the hour of the wolf," it is easy to believe that we are still waiting to appear. I once heard of a man who was such a nonentity that when he was drowning, someone else's life flashed before his eyes.

This helps me understand what Jesus meant when He said to His disciples, "I have set you an example." He did not mean that we should slavishly imitate Him, but that we should so follow His example as to catch His spirit; and should so hear His voice as to find our own.

In the early twenties, George Gershwin went off to the Paris of Hemingway, Joyce, Copland, and Virgil Thompson, hoping to study orchestration with Maurice Ravel. But Ravel, who knew Gershwin's work, was wiser than Gershwin and would have none of it: "Better a first-rate Gershwin than a second-rate Ravel," he said.

That is how Lady Day and Pres found their voice, and never sang louder than lovely, though their song was sad and short.

In a glowing sentence that holds in itself both the work and the grace of creativity, Emily Dickinson wrote, "Art is a house that tries to be haunted." I used to think it would have been better if she had said, "Art is a house that *waits* to be haunted"; but I was wrong; for the haunting is impossible without the work, commitment, and passion of the trying.

Any artist who is more than a mere doodler will build the house by mastering the clay or paint or words or notes that are the stuff of craft and by learning the tricks of the trade, its techniques, devices, and stratagems. The artist may then dare to hope that one day the Spirit will come like a ghost and haunt the house, elevating the work above mere self-expression and imparting to it a universal significance.

Charles Mingus is strange company for the Belle of Amherst, but he would have agreed with her in this. Mingus treated with fierce contempt those exponents of free jazz who aspired to be original before they had learned their notes, and thought themselves avant-garde before they had mastered their instruments. He had no respect for the charlatans who wanted the haunting without the trying. Mingus thought of free jazz as Robert Frost thought of free verse: it was like playing tennis with the net down. Mingus used to say, "You can't improvise on nothin', man. You gotta improvise on somethin'."

It is one of God's little jokes that those who try to be original usually fail even to be interesting. Truly original thinkers do not think about being original, but get on with their work. It is not originality they're after, but truth, clarity, insight. If they prove to be original, their originality is theirs by what has been called "The Principle of Inattention." Like joy, originality surprises them when they are doing something else or looking the other way. Originality is not something they aim at; it is where their work takes them and where the road leads.

When Dennis Potter, the most gifted and startling writer in the history of television drama, was asked about his astonishing innovations, his habit of breaking the mold—as when he had children in *Those Blue Remembered Hills* played by adults—he replied that he had never thought of breaking anything. He had done what he needed to do in order to say what he wished to say. His innovations were not something he decided to bring in, having just thought of them; they were what his work required and were necessary to his craft. All of which means that we all need somewhere to begin.

Art Tatum was a jazz pianist whose technical brilliance and dazzling mastery of harmonic and rhythmic inventiveness overwhelmed all who heard him. When he was criticized for relying heavily on popular tunes for his material, he replied that jazz is not about where you start from but about where you can go. Whatever else it did, his choice of popular tunes such as "Danny Boy" and "Mighty Like A Rose" acknowledged his indebtedness to others. Everything he did had about it a sense of discovery and adventure, as though he were saying to us, "Now, let's see where this will take us!" But Tatum knew he was a guest of existence, that he had received "the unbought grace of life." He went on from there, as *The New York Times* put it, "to show us what it is like to live in a world where all doors are open."

We improvise on what others have handed to us. One medieval teacher used to tell his scholars that we are dwarfs mounted on

The Fine Art of Being Imperfect

the shoulders of giants. If we know more than our ancestors, it is because our ancestors are what we know. The jazz musician, like the poet, may become a prophet only because he dwells in a tradition he did not create and eats at a table he did not spread.

Improvisation must begin in respect, and innovation in the given. Freedom should be the expression of restraint, and spontaneity the gift of sureness, and pragmatism the application of principle. Yeats, in "The Second Coming," tells us that when it is otherwise,

> Things fall apart; the center cannot hold;
> Mere anarchy is loosed upon the world,
> The blood-dimmed tide is loosed, and everywhere
> The ceremony of innocence is drowned;
> The best lack all conviction, while the worst
> Are full of passionate intensity.

Mingus and Tatum were right: "You can't improvise on nothin' man, you gotta improvise on somethin'."

One dare not speak of jazz without recognizing the enormous cost of it. I added up the ages of ten of the great ones, and divided by ten, and had a figure of thirty years. Lester Young died at fifty, which is an advanced old age for a jazz musician; John Coltrane at forty; Charlie Parker at thirty-four.

One reason for these musicians' early deaths was their lifestyle; their apparent death wish of self-neglect, strong drink, drugs, and prison. Another reason was that they lived what they played: as Charlie Parker put it, "If you don't live it, it won't come out of your horn." Those who are good at it soon discover that jazz is both a rich gift of God and a burden heavy to be borne. They are like the poet described by Kierkegaard, who suffers deeply but is so made that the sounds of his anguish are beautiful to hear. They are such an enchantment to those who listen to them that they cry out for more, thus inviting the poet to suffer further for their sake.

Yet the cost is greater even than that, for jazz is the sound of Black America, and is therefore the sorrow of a people—their oppression, despair, and longing—finding utterance in music of overwhelming power and immediacy. And because that is what it is, it is also the song of triumph of the human spirit. No less splendidly than that glorious distant trumpet in Beethoven's *Fidelio,* Louis Armstrong's trumpet and Charlie Parker's sax announce deliverance.

The miracle of jazz is that when on the twelfth day of February, 1924, in New York City, American music came of age and sang the song it came to sing, the color of the composition was Blue and the nature of it a Rhapsody.

The Fine Art of Being Imperfect

10

RUNNING
TO JUDGMENT

Does it bother you that God knows your secrets?

When I was a child, I was taught what the Scriptures teach; that God is the One who knows, judges, and reveals the secrets of our hearts. This knowledge would be openly declared and God's verdict delivered on the Day of Judgment. As it was assumed that all secrets, even those of childish hearts, were guilty secrets, Judgment Day became the stuff of nightmares; a terrifying day of shocking revelations, acute embarrassment, fierce condemnation, and overwhelming horror. How the spirit sickened and shriveled at the thought of it!

Please notice that this appalling prospect need not be read into the actual words of Scripture; yet there were always those who would load the Scriptures up with enough nasty ideas to ensure that God's knowledge and revealing of our secrets was a prospect to be dreaded. To this day I know by heart a chorus such persons used to sing:

> Oh, how sad it will be,
> On that Great Judgment morning,
> To be cast out of heaven
> For not loving God!

The most menacing texts of Scripture were chosen to strengthen the case and were not only preached in church but painted on signs along the highway. I can see them still: "It is appointed unto man once to die, and after that, the Judgment" they said; along with another sign, "The Wages of Sin is Death."

A woman I knew went so far as to have one of these unhappy verses made into a sign that she mounted on the roof of her car: "Prepare to meet Thy God!" it announced to every approaching motorist. A friend of mine suggested that the urgency of her advice was occasioned by the recklessness of her driving. He thought it considerate of her to give us such clear and timely warning.

All that God knew of us came from information that had been taken down to be used as evidence against us. It consisted, for the most part, of knowing how bad we were. It was written indelibly in a Great Book that would be opened and read aloud on the Last Day of the world to titillate every trivial mind, indulge every incorrigible gossip, and embarrass anyone with an ounce of sensitivity.

Now, this telling of our secrets might seem an appalling breach of confidence on God's part; but it was all right for Him to do it, because He was God. It was therefore inappropriate to despise Him for it, as we would a friend whom we found guilty of such treachery. In God's case the safest thing to do was to praise and adore Him, ascribing worth to behavior we should find contemptible in anyone else.

We had thought all our confessions safe, only to discover that they had been saved up to become the substance of an Apocalyptic Day on which everything would be revealed and everyone learn the shameful things that had been intended for God's ears only. This meant, of course, that divine judgment was really the ultimate condemnation. Nor could there be any appeal to a higher court, for no one is higher than God.

The Fine Art of Being Imperfect

The guilty verdict was followed by a sentence of eternal punishment: everlasting separation from God by God's own decree. It seemed immoderate to punish temporal sins with eternal torment; this was surely a most indelicate balance, for it was hard to imagine any wickedness heinous enough to warrant such prolonged misery. And besides, there was no point to it, for the blessed did not need it and the damned could not profit by it.

Little wonder, then, that some declared the arrangement immoral and turned from faith because of it. Charles Darwin was one of them. It was not Darwin's science that drove him from faith, but his theology. He refused to believe what he called the "damnable doctrine" that those whom he most loved and honored would be condemned and consigned to everlasting suffering. Only the righteous seemed satisfied with this ordering of things. Who were the righteous? Why, those who knew they were, and told us so.

This pattern of Divine judgment quickly became the model for our own. How well I remember a woman who told me of an incident in the church where she had been brought up. She described how one young girl, charged with fornication, was tried in the face of the whole congregation, found guilty, and expelled—her minister being her chief accuser. No wonder Albert Camus said that he did not fear the Divine judgment, for he had experienced the judgment of men, and God's could not be worse.

The plot thickened when every painter, composer, and poet, believer and unbeliever alike, discovered that the judgment of God is the stuff of drama and found the subject irresistible. Imagine it painted on an enormous wall! What a spectacle it would make on the stage at La Scala! They proceeded to heighten the horror by their paintings, plays, and poems; and with a flourish of last trumps announced that it was too late to flee from the wrath to come.

The judgment of God need not be understood in the terrible way we have described. Indeed, even as a child I sensed deeply that there was something wrong with the things I was being told; that the goodness of God could not be as bad as it sounded. I knew, without knowing that I knew, how even God must suffer at the hands of His interpreters; that small men would make God small, and that cruel men would fashion Him after their own image. Since then, I have discovered how much truth there may be in a child's intuition.

What if God's perfect knowledge of our hearts is not the reason for His condemnation of us, but the measure of His intimacy with us? The Scriptures tell us that God knows us at the depth of our groaning. If He does, then it must mean that He knows us better than we know ourselves, for our groans are, of their very nature, inarticulate. They are wrung from us when we do not understand and cannot express the depth of what we feel—when the mystery of our own heart bewilders us.

But if God knows our hearts better than we do, it means that He can read between our lines, understand our silences, and take the meaning that is often hidden behind our words. Indeed, He speaks with the voice we cannot find and pleads for us with a longing we cannot express. In this way He satisfies our desire to be acknowledged, understood, and accepted.

There are always those who think they can read us like a book, but the wise and loving ones, when reading us, know that we are something different from what they read. Simone Weil expresses it beautifully when she tells us that every being cries out to be read differently; that is, to be read truly. Those who presume to read us like a book are, for the most part, reading fiction. They are like Hamlet's naive acquaintances who cannot sound even the few notes of a simple recorder, yet imagine they can play all the music of his being. We are not as easily read, or played, as they suppose.

The Fine Art of Being Imperfect

We may go even further and say that God, who knows us better than we know ourselves and reads us truly, tells our secrets, not to embarrass us before others, but to interpret us to ourselves. The secrets of God's revealing are not so much ours as His: what He has always known about us and now shows to us, as we are able to bear it. It is not that we have discovered these things and entrusted them to Him; but that He has always known them, and discloses them to us. In this way this Teller of Secrets brings us to ourselves.

We may well shrink from such knowledge; but when we do, it is not because God is wrathful but because what He knows is the truth, and truth may be painful. He is a brave man indeed who does not shrink from it, for none of us can bear very much reality. Yet the best and deepest part of us longs, not only to know and bear truth, but also to be reconciled to it. For who among us would wish to remain false when we might be honest; or avert our gaze from that which, sooner or later, we must not only acknowledge but embrace? We know that to turn away forever from truth and reality is to suffer an enduring loss: to be eternally unreal, everlastingly untrue. Ask any psychiatrist.

That is why the soul, no longer wishing to flee from the wrath to come, will, in Plato's splendid words, "Go running to judgment"—not only dreading but desiring it—knowing that the flame that burns is the fire that refines, the truth that pierces is the reality that heals, the brightness that exposes is the light by which we see. Languishing in shadows, and weary of the half light and the half life, we long for the truth of everlasting day.

We have forgotten that it is God who judges us. We have thereby separated the Divine judgment from the Divine character and distorted our every thought about a Day of Judgment. Our mistake has even allowed us, when we have so wished, to falsify the nature of God's judgment by our cruelest imaginings.

We should remember that the quality of God's judgment will be determined, not by our pettiness, but by His greatness; not by our meanness, but by the Divine generosity; not by the miserable little demons of anger, envy, inferiority and self-righteousness that so frequently torment our human spirits, but by the inexhaustible kindness and mercy of the Spirit of God.

We made God's knowledge of us into a sinister, trivial, and sordid kind of knowing, forgetting that His understanding of us is what perfect wisdom shares with perfect love. We accused Him of betraying our secrets, when all He wished to reveal to us was the mystery of our heart and the tenderness of His own. We took His wrath to be like our own blind fury, when it was nothing but His goodness setting itself against us, for our good. We were so eager to see the wicked get their comeuppance that we made God's judgment an extension of our own exasperation; forgetting that we, too, live by the Divine injustice that does not immediately afflict us by giving us what we deserve.

Paul tells us that on the Day of Judgment, "God will judge the secrets of men's hearts by Christ Jesus." This means that nothing will happen that is alien to the Spirit of Christ. It was Jesus who taught us that God is not to be feared, but loved; that we should call Him, *Abba,* Father, Daddy, because God thinks of us, and loves us, as His children. We should allow that truth to refine our every thought of God's judgment.

I know a first-rate theologian who did so. He loved to tell how one day, when still a child, he disobeyed his mother and was sent to his room to wait until his father came home. It seemed that ages passed before he heard his father's key in the front door. There were sounds of greeting, and then muffled conversation in which, he supposed, the story of his wickedness was told. The suspense was more than he could bear; so thinking it better to meet judgment halfway, he left his room and started down the stairs. He had descended only a little way when his father appeared, caught sight of him, rushed to meet him, and gathered him into his arms with the words, "My own wee son!" For the rest of his life he was to remember what he called "the delicious sense of belonging to my father." He could never speak of it without tears in his eyes. When the thought of judgment appalls, we may remember that our Judge is our Father who created us, and to whom we belong.

But Paul meant more even than this; for this Christ who judges the world is the Savior who came into the world for our sake, wedding Himself to us beyond any separation and loving us to death with every drop of His life. This Jesus by whom we are judged knows our humanity as One who shares it; for He still carries in His dazzling Body the dear tokens of our nature, the wounds of His passion, the scars of His suffering. Was there ever such a Judge as this, who "hath given us joy by His sorrow and life by His death"?

11

DREAM CHILDREN

If you wanted to discover your soul, would you know what you were looking for and where to find it?

When I was in theological college, the study across the hall was occupied by a medical student who didn't think much of the budding theologians who surrounded him. The reason for his antipathy was that he didn't believe in the soul. He liked to say that he had dissected many a cadaver without finding a soul, and had concluded that all talk of it was emptiness and chasing the wind.

I asked him one day if he had ever discovered personality, or encountered character, or cut into temperament, or consciousness, or spirit while dividing lifeless things; and if he had surrendered belief in their reality along with his belief in the soul. But he had delivered his best line and considered it fine enough to make further comment unnecessary.

The poor fellow failed his year and had to give up medicine and find something else to study. I think he turned to engineering. This was a great disappointment to him, but it may have been a kindness to the patients who would have come under his care. I mean, who would wish to be treated by a soulless physician whose second choice was engineering?

He may have been just a little ahead of his time, though, for the people most likely to mention the soul nowadays are those who think of it as a kind of "ghostly other" that each of us has but is in danger of losing. They would like to save it for us. Some preachers I heard when I was growing up were known for their "passion for souls," which meant that they *really* wanted to save them. I fought them every inch, for I thought they were more interested in my soul than they were in me. It was a scalp to be lifted, a notch on their gun, a number to add to the statistics of their success and the magnitude of their reputation. My soul was a star in their crown, so that I was never sure if they wanted to save it for my sake or their own. Because of them I came to regard the soul with distaste and wished I did not have one.

There was a time, though, when people spoke easily and naturally of the soul, and knew what they meant by it, and were understood when they mentioned it. I looked the word up in *Bartlett's Familiar Quotations* and discovered that sayings containing it filled six columns. "Spirit" filled three, while "Body" and "Flesh" managed a meager one and a half columns each. It seems that the most quotable thinkers of the past could best describe us, not as material, or even as bodily creatures, but as souls or spirits. They made us more real by making us less tangible.

They knew, for one thing, that although we have bodies we are not to be identified with them. I occupy a body, which I have no wish to diminish, for it is an essential part of the person I am. I could not think what I am saying or say what I am thinking without it. But my body is not me, nor am I to be discovered in any part of it. You will not find me in my arm or leg or heart—or brain, even. I am everywhere present and nowhere to be found. I may be identified *by* my body, recognized by its height, weight, and particular configurations; but I cannot be identified *with* it, for it is not me, but mine. I speak of my brain, my hair, and the color of my eyes. But who is this "I" behind the "my," and where is this person to be found who presides over everything?

Our grandparents knew. When they spoke of the soul they meant this vital, enlivening, animating spirit that is the self. They had no difficulty believing that God is a Spirit, for they were themselves spirits who could commune with Him, "spirit to Spirit." The soul was the self, the true and innermost self, the self Whitman called "thou actual me."

You don't *possess* a soul, you *are* a soul; you don't *have* a spirit, you *are* a spirit. Your soul is you, the thinking, feeling, animating element in your intellectual and emotional life. To speak of you without mentioning spirit would be like defining an orchestra without mentioning music.

If we are spirits, then to describe us as material substance is to use terms too substantial for their work. Airier words are needed for the sort of stuff we are, as our poets and musicians have always known. So they have devised a lightsome vocabulary of words and notes, calling us "Dream Children," for we are "nothing, and less than nothing, and dreams." Shakespeare wrote:

> These our actors . . .
> were all spirits and
> Are melted into air, into thin air . . .
> . . . We are such stuff
> As dreams are made on, and our little life
> Is rounded with a sleep.

If the soul is the self, then it makes perfect sense to say that it may be lost. But losing our soul is not like losing our credit card; it is not that we suddenly miss it and try to remember the last time we used it or where we might have left it. To lose one's soul is not to misplace something that belongs to us; it is to betray our deepest sense of self.

It has been the business of every serious playwright in the history of the world to remind us of this by setting the drama of it in front of our eyes. They know that because character matters supremely, the real battles are always about keeping or losing the self. The nobler the self at risk, the greater the tension of its

The Fine Art of Being Imperfect

conflict and the deeper the tragedy should it fall. It is the nobility of Othello that makes the pity of Othello, for we cannot bear to look on while so admirable a spirit is destroyed.

Whatever the other props and bits of scenery, the true setting of all tragic drama is a moral expectation, an ethical demand, a requirement of conscience, which the self must fulfill or else be lost. Lacking this, the plays hold little interest. As Chesterton put it, "Books without morality in them are books that will send you to sleep standing up."

Robert Bolt has his *Man for All Seasons* explain this to his daughter Margaret when she pleads with him to secure his release from prison by swearing an oath he does not mean: "When a man takes an oath, Meg, he's holding his own self in his own hands. Like water. And if he opens his fingers—he needn't hope to find himself again." Sir Thomas More chose not to open his fingers, and died rather than "put his hand on an old black book and tell an ordinary lie."

We have spoken of our spirit: the animating element of our person, the vitality of our thought, the energy of our feeling, the strength of our willing. This spirit pervades our being as our breath permeates our body, quickening it with verve and vigor.

Yet breath is not the only image that expresses the nature of spirit. The image of breath helps us understand the spirit's inwardness and grasp the meaning of the soul; but the spirit has other likenesses to capture its inexhaustible variety of forms and innumerable accomplishments.

What if the Spirit (capital "S" this time) not only constitutes the self but carries us out of the self, bears us beyond the self, and imparts to the self what is not in the self: quickening our energies, heightening our perception, refining our feeling, enlightening our understanding, and granting us eloquent utterance! This is what it means to be inspired, to be "in-breathed"; to not only catch God's breath but feel the Wind of the Creator and Creative Spirit. D. H. Lawrence cried, "Not I, Not I, but the wind that blows through me!"

All true artists feel these freshening breezes and lift their sail to catch them. Hemingway did when he said, "Most of the time I write as well as I can; occasionally I write better." Robert Frost spoke of "the surprise of remembering something I didn't know I knew"; and a friend of mine, a young woman whom I encouraged to become a minister, wrote to tell me that last Sunday she preached better than she can preach.

Singers know when they are no longer carrying a tune but are being carried on wings of song. Dancers discover with delight that their limbs are clothed with grace, accomplishing without effort what they have struggled to attain. Writers sometimes wish they could write with both hands so as to capture all the words that crowd and clamor for expression. Actors cherish the performances when their lines come to them already possessed, and poised, and eloquent. Composers live for the moment when the air is "Full of sounds and sweet airs that give delight and hurt not."

Any artist who is more than a mere doodler knows such occasions; and so do we. Whether we are accountants or lawyers or homemakers or teachers or physicians or money managers, there come to us "moments of glad grace" when we are granted an unusual degree of sureness and insight. We, too, feel the Winds of God, and lift our sail.

Emily Dickinson tells us, in a glowing sentence, that "Art is a house that tries to be haunted," for the Creator Spirit is the Holy Ghost. She encourages us to build our structure; to master the words or notes, the paint or numbers, the tricks of our trade with its devices and stratagems; and then to hope that one day the Spirit will come to haunt our house and elevate our work to a universal significance. The Spirit's gift is not only the beauty of filled sails, but the charm of magic casements:

The Fine Art of Being Imperfect

> And so the shadows fall apart
> And so the West Winds play.
> And all the windows of my heart
> I open to Thy day.

The Wind of the Spirit is more playful than the west winds ever were. Imagine its making the apostles look a little tipsy at Pentecost! This breeze does more than lift our skirt or snatch away our hat or blow our umbrella inside out: it bends our rigidity and gives our stiffness its dismission; it sends our pomposity swirling and wafts us gifts of originality, spontaneity and improvisation. Thelonious Monk called himself "Sphere" because he had no wish to be square, and even *Harper's Bazaar* knows that to avoid middle age we should get heavily into jazz.

Jesus said that the Spirit is like the wind—mysterious and invisible, but easily recognized by what it does. We cannot see it, but we know where it is by the tossing waves or driving rain or moving clouds, or by having it dry the washing or fly a kite. Rossetti asks:

> Who has seen the wind?
>   Neither I nor you:
> But when the leaves hang trembling,
>   The wind is passing through.

> Who has seen the wind?
>   Neither you nor I:
> But when the trees bow down their heads,
>   The wind is passing by.

In a similar way, the Spirit is like a good pair of eyeglasses. If our eyeglasses fit comfortably and do their work well we hardly notice them. They are there, not to be noticed, but to enable us to notice. They are not to be seen, but to be seen through. When we misplace them we are doubly troubled, for we have not only lost them, but cannot see to find them. To search for the Spirit is like looking for our glasses while wearing them—one of God's little jokes.

If we wish to claim inspiration by the Spirit, then, should we point at the Spirit or to the truth He has revealed? If, by His quickening, our young men have seen visions and our old men dreamed dreams, should we investigate the Spirit or catch the vision and share the dreams? If a composer begins his work with the words, "Come, Creator Spirit," how shall we discover if his prayer has been answered: by examining the Spirit, or by listening to his music?

The Fine Art of Being Imperfect

12

ON SEEING THROUGH PEOPLE

Are you clever enough to see through people?

If we claim to see through people it should be a claim to see them clearly, for that is the only way to see. And sometimes we do truly see others by seeing through them. Those who practice to deceive do not deceive us, for we're "on to them" and are not tricked by appearances. Looks can be misleading, for one "may smile, and smile, and be a villain," but we are not taken in. We are nobody's fool. We pride ourselves on it.

That is how Jesus of Nazareth saw through people. He knew them well enough not to trust Himself to some of them. He longed for followers as shrewd in their understanding of evil as the wicked were who lived by it. He set no premium on naïveté.

Seeing through others in this way will offend those who espouse the "I'm OK, You're OK" view of our nature, for they see no evil in anything. Here we have the three little monkeys over again, freshened up with a dash of pop psychology. How naively they underestimate our capacity for mischief, and how grossly overestimate the content of our character!

Not many years ago, grown men and women stood in front of their morning mirror, looked their drowsy reflections more or less straight in the eye, and attempted to convince themselves that "every day, in every way [they were] getting better and better."

How did they manage to keep a straight face? Why did their sense of humor not break in to save them from their silliness? It didn't, though; so undeterred, and with a little help from Darwin, they persuaded themselves that everything was on the up-and-up—inevitably, irresistibly, everywhere, and all the time.

We had thought that all such fantasies of human perfectibility perished in the Holocaust and the Gulag, that we had learned from experience that evil is universal, pervasive, and intractable. But old heresies never die and seldom fade away. They just assume another form.

Some churches, even, fearful that any mention of imperfection might offend the unfaithful, decided never to bring it up. They smoothed out their gospel until it became the story of how "a God without wrath brought men without sin into a Kingdom without judgment, through the ministrations of a Christ without a cross." Worship ended, home the happy parishioners went, equipped by the power of positive thinking to pursue their perfect ends by perfect means in their best of all possible worlds.

How like dear Walt Whitman they were, who thought he might like to go and live with the animals, who do not lie awake in the dark and weep for their sins. He didn't, though, for the animals who do not confess their sins do not read his poetry, either. Being animals, they're not big on either penitence or literary appreciation. Our mea culpa, far from giving us a reason to join them, raises us a cut above them as responsible creatures who not only have lost their innocence, but live in a world of moral expectation.

Thank God for the editors, dramatists, poets, and novelists who kept their wits about them and saw through this nonsense. For Richard Crossman, for example, who considered the state of the world and concluded that there is more to be said for the doctrine of original sin than for Rousseau's idea of the Noble Savage; the Noble Savage having proved more savage than noble.

Ogden Nash told us that progress was once a good idea but has been going on too long. Edna St. Vincent Millay called it the dirtiest word in the language, for it means impetus without direction—rather like running in the dark.

82   *The Fine Art of Being Imperfect*

Seeing through others is a bit of a fraud in another sense; for the righteous indignation it arouses is often a pose, being more indignant than righteous and closer to self-righteousness than we care to admit. The truth is that we are not better than the people we see through. The only safe way to become proficient in seeing through others is to practice on ourselves. Others will be less able to take us in when we are not self-deceived to begin with.

The greatest difficulty with seeing through things is so obvious that we easily overlook it: if we see through everything we shall soon be unable to see anything, for our whole world will have become transparent.

Most things are meant, not to be seen through, but to be seen. Windows are an exception, of course, and glasses and telescopes and microscopes. We look through them in order to see something else: flowers in the garden or small print or distant stars. But if we see through everything, if the whole world is transparent, there isn't anything left to see.

Have pity on the devil then, who so cleverly sees through everything that he sees nothing. Shed a tear for poor Mephistopheles, who having eyes to see, sees not; and having ears to hear, hears not the sounds of sweet harmony that float divinely even in his discordant world.

There is another way of seeing through people that is unlike anything I have mentioned. It will neither protect us against deception nor expose the unhappy limitations of others. Instead, it gets under their skin in such a way as to experience reality as they perceive it.

Carved over the entrance to the philosophy department of a great university are the words, "Settle into the mind of Plato, and think from there." That is an invitation not only to think like Plato, but also to see "through Plato."

Now that's a pretty tall order, but Plato would have loved it and might well have thought it an informed attempt to do him justice. Both Plato and Aristotle describe justice as giving to every man what is his due, and that means making an imaginative effort to see the world as he sees it. Justice would be well served if we could borrow for a while the eyes of those we wish to know and need to understand: If men could see as women see, and management as labor; if Whites could view the world through the eyes of Blacks and parents become children again, as they do for a little while at Christmas.

Lovers do it all the time. When we care deeply for someone, our world is no longer narrowly ours, for we begin to see it through their eyes, interpret it in their interest, shape it to their liking, and hedge it for their safety. We die a little to ourselves by seeing "through them." That is what the poet meant who told us that to know the meaning of love is to learn the meaning of death.

That is the nature of religious faith. Faith is not something to be seen, merely, but a way of seeing. We see through it and interpret everything in the light of it. It is more than turning to the church advertisements in the local paper or the religion columns of *Time* or *Newsweek*. It is a way of taking the world spread out for us on all the pages in every section. Our failure of faith is that for all our scrutiny of it, we have not made it our way of perceiving, doing, and loving.

When I sing that great Irish hymn "Be Thou My Vision, O Lord of My Heart," my prayer is that God should be not only before my eyes, but in them—the Vision I see, and the vision that is my power of seeing.

It happened to Dante. For an instant he saw the whole order of things through the eyes of God, felt it with Divine sorrow, held it in redeeming love, and embraced it with transcendent joy:

> I saw gathered in one volume, bound by love, all the scattered leaves of the universe; fused after such fashion that all which I tell is one simple flame. The universal form of this complex whole I think that I saw, because as I say this I feel my joy increasing.

The Fine Art of Being Imperfect

13

TURTLES ALL
THE WAY DOWN

*Does the vastness of the universe make you feel
bigger or smaller?*

Stephen Hawking wrote a book called *A Brief History of Time,* which everybody bought, most people started, and hardly anyone finished or understood.

He begins it with the story of a young philosopher who delivered a public lecture on the nature and origin of the universe. He spoke of incredible spans of time and unimaginable distances, and the relation between them. When he had finished, a little old lady stood up and said, "Young man, everything you have told us this evening is rubbish. The earth is a flat plate resting on the back of a giant tortoise." The philosopher took her in his stride. Smiling confidently, and only a little condescendingly, he asked, "But Madam, on what does the turtle rest?" Unabashed, the little old lady continued to talk plain talk: "You are a clever young man," she said, "very clever indeed; but it's turtles all the way down."

Two explanations; and notice that each is as remote from our experience as the other. Why do we assume that our best clues will be found long ago and far away, forgetting that creation is not over, but is going on all the time, and that the mystery of existence is first encountered neither far out nor far back, but in deep, in our awareness of ourselves and the world in which we live and move and have our being? Not there and then, but here and now; not in the first three minutes, but in this moment; not in turtles all the way down, but in the words I am writing and you are reading, for neither you nor I will be exactly the same when this chapter is finished. Creation isn't over. The beat goes on!

Israel's understanding of creation began in present experience. Those who wrote the creation stories in the first chapters of Genesis were not superscientists, but poets and prophets who spoke of that Creator Spirit who was more present to them than their deepest consciousness of self, as pervasive as their own breath, as unavoidable as conscience, as instant as intuition. They said that this Spirit, who intimately formed and informed them, had created the stars. The God who spoke to them in their own conscience was the Maker of all things visible and invisible. This conclusion might easily seem a claim too large for too little evidence, yet the prophets of Israel had good reason for their conviction.

For one thing, they knew that to make us, God had to create a world. This ought not to surprise us when we consider that to make a loaf of bread God had to make the world. When I am asked to say grace at meals, I sometimes repeat the lovely words of Maltbie Babcock:

> Back of the loaf is the snowy flour,
> And back of the flour the mill;
> And back of the mill is the wheat and the shower,
> And the sun, and the Father's will.

The poem tells us that the whole universe is in a loaf; the sun in every apple and the moon in every bunch of grapes. And the whole universe is in you and me. For us to exist, God had to create everything in which our being is grounded. To make us, God had to make the stuff of which we are made.

The truth is, of course, that we are made of stardust. When I say this, I am not reciting poetry or uttering a religious sentiment, but telling a literal truth. Our earth is a fragment of an exploded star, so that you and I, made of the dust of the earth, have been fashioned from stardust. To make us, God first had to form the stars of which we are made.

Not long ago, a young couple I know announced the birth of their son by sending cards on which were printed an excerpt from George MacDonald's "Where Did You Come From, Baby Dear?"

> Where did you come from, baby dear?
> Out of the Everywhere into the here.
> Where did you get your eyes so blue?
> Out of the sky as I came through.

MacDonald was exactly right. He expresses the truth poetically, but there are facts behind his verse. If there is no Everywhere, there is no here. If there are no blue skies, there can be no blue eyes, nor brown eyes either, for that matter. If no stars twinkle, no eyes will shine. No galaxies, no gaiety. No milky way, no path for our feet. To make us, God had to put rain on the wind, and cloud-shadows on the hills: cast rainbows over the sun, and wash the world with moonbeams.

In "The Valley of Wild Thyme," Sidney Lysaght has a child ask his mother what it takes to make a rose. Her answer is that a rose is not possible without the moon and the stars, and the world's eternal wars:

> It takes the might of Heaven and Hell
> And the Everlasting Love as well, little child.

If that is what it takes to make a rose, it cannot have taken less to make us.

We should notice an objection to this way of thinking: an objection that has been around for a very long time, and which made a recent appearance in *The Toronto Globe and Mail* when an English astrophysicist wrote an article taking Stephen Hawking to task for speaking of "knowing the mind of God" as he sought to discover the meaning of the universe. This scientist said that the universe has no meaning and no purpose. Life and human intelligence exist by "chance." We are not here except by chance.

Now, what is this "chance" by which we are brought to life and being? The English scientist speaks of it as though it were a grand design, an all-embracing purpose that guides and directs and is the reason for everything. Some chance! I have always thought that chance is the absence of intentional action. It isn't an explanation; it is the absence of explanation. Now, suddenly, we are told that chance creates, explains, and is responsible for everything. I think such a way of talking is nonsense.

I can prove it to you. Suppose I were to describe a social event, say a wedding I attended: I might say that the catering was by H & H Bagels, the groom's suit by L. L. Bean, the bride's gown by Eddie Bauer, and the music by the Orpheus Chamber Orchestra. So far, so good! But suppose I then went on to say that the bride's hair was styled "by chance." What would you make of that? You would conclude that the bride's hair was in state of disarray. Chance cannot style anything; yet here we are, calmly attributing the universe to something that couldn't arrange a young woman's hairdo!

I know a historian who says that chance is a mask and that it is precisely the historian's duty to lift it off or tear it away, for it explains nothing. The historian does much better than the astrophysicist, but the poet says it even better.

Hear, for example, Whitman's *Leaves of Grass:*

> O vast Rondure, swimming in space,
> Covered all over with visible power and beauty;

> With inscrutable purpose,
> Some hidden prophetic intention,
> Now first it seems my thought begins to span thee!

To make us, God had to create a world. To create the world, God had to make us.

Another reason why we ought not to think of creation as something that happened long ago is that we have part in it. The Creator Spirit has given us creative spirits to share with Him in His work and play of creation. In making the world, God didn't compose all the symphonies, paint all the pictures, pen all the poems, write all the plays. That is why this world is always unfinished, forever incomplete.

Dylan Thomas once said that every great poem has gaps in it, "Where a man's own meaning may creep, crawl, flash or thunder in." And the world is like that. It is as open-ended as our imagination, as unfinished as our hopes, as spacious as our dreams.

T. H. White expresses this splendidly in *The Sword and the Stone.* All the little embryos are gathered before God to receive from Him any gift they might wish to claim. The badger asks for claws, and the tiger for fangs. Some want shells for their protection, while others ask for wings. The antelope covets fleetness of foot, and the fish ask for fins by which to pursue and escape. Then comes the turn of an embryo who has been watching and listening very carefully. He asks for nothing except that God should make Him in His image, with the power to think, and love, and know himself. He says that if he needs to swim he'll build him a boat; if he needs to fly he will make himself wings. He will erect his own house for shelter and forge his own weapons for defense. And when he has finished his asking, God is well pleased, and tells him that he has chosen well. Then, as the first human leaves the Divine Presence, God calls after him, "God bless you!"

God did not compose Mozart's *Clarinet Concerto;* He created Mozart and inspired him to compose it. God did not create

Othello or Lear of Falstaff; He made Shakespeare and put him to work. And so it is with you and me. Our spirits are touched to creativity by the Creator Spirit, who makes His world using creatures who are themselves still in the making.

What an elevation of the human spirit that is! Pascal tells us that even if the universe were to crush us, we are greater than the universe, for we would know it and the universe would not. However vast the universe, our human spirit transcends it, filling the vastnesses of space, greater than stars or suns, measuring time and life and death, encompassing them all by our thought.

To make us, God created a world; to make a world, God created us. The Creator, then, is not less personal than those He has created.

People sometimes tell me that they believe in "Something," with a capital "S," but that they don't believe in a personal God, thus denying God the attributes, qualities, and values that make us personal: thought, will, intention, self-awareness, love, creativity, humor, freedom. Such talk is silly, for if God does not possess these qualities, He is less personal than we are, which means He is no God at all. That kind of explanation explains nothing. It is like saying that Mickey Mouse is more personal than Walt Disney; that Hamlet is greater than Shakespeare; that there is more life in Tiny Tim than there is in Charles Dickens; more intelligence in the muppets than in Jim Hensen.

No one knew this better than Robert Frost. In an amusing poem called "Accidentally on Purpose" he writes:

> Grant me intention, purpose and design—
> That's near enough for me to the Divine.

It's near enough for me, too.

Grant me intention, purpose and design, and I'll give you, not only a personal God, but a world charged with His grandeur and filled with His praise.

14

DREAMS TO SELL

Are you too ambitious, or not ambitious enough?

I'd like to examine the nature of ambition. I'll begin by noticing how hard it is to get it right. Everybody we know has either too much or too little of it. The trouble with Harry, we say, is that, having too much, he's always overreaching and getting himself into trouble; while George has never been ambitious enough, so that the song he came to sing remains unsung.

Finding the right amount of ambition may be uncertain; but there is no mistaking the enormous energy it releases, not only to the personal advantage of those who have it, but to the benefit of all.

Ambition teaches us to cherish the other values needed to sustain and fulfill it—qualities of initiative, independence, imagination, courage, perseverance, discipline, sacrifice. My goodness there's hardly a quality to be thought of that is not gathered into its enterprises!

Ambition is the very condition of individual achievement; and it is the genius of our free enterprise system that it unashamedly acknowledges this, blesses it, and seeks to direct its energies to the common good.

Yet while we are right to praise ambition, we must be careful not to praise it overmuch, for it can easily get out of hand and turn demonic. It can be selfish and savage, raw and ruthless, lacking in compassion and devoid of conscience. It then becomes the weapon of greed and the cause of much misery.

When ambition becomes unscrupulous, it is guilty of a deplorable act of betrayal. Its loss of principle has about it a stench of treason, for it threatens the very system that allows it to be. Its moral failure begins in a sort of treachery that bites the hand that feeds it and treats with contempt the liberty that makes it possible.

Now, if it is so hard for us to get ambition right, and if in the same breath we must praise its achievements and lament its excesses, we really should keep one eye on it to keep it honest, and to be aware of what it is doing to us and through us. So let me ask four questions to keep our ambition wholesome.

1. What is it you're after?

One of the loveliest poems in our language is "Dream Pedlary" by Thomas Beddoes. It asks:

> If there were dreams to sell,
> What would you buy?

The Mossad, the Israeli Secret Service, knows that there *are* dreams to sell, and knows which dreams we buy. They tell us that they can get to almost anybody by one, or some combination, of three things: power, sex, and money. These, then, are the things we are after, the stuff of our dreams.

Someone once remarked that we can tell the quality of our culture by the nature of its advertisements. Our commercials display the things we want, announcing our values, exposing our hungers, and pandering to our fantasies. Oh, dear! This means that the subway will not only carry us to our work; its advertisements will tell us why we are going! Or think of Las Vegas at night! Or of Times Square when the lights go on! G. K. Chesterton was asked what he thought of it, and he replied that it would be wonderful if you couldn't read.

> If there were dreams to sell,
> What would you buy?

What is it *you're* after?
This brings us to the second question.

2. Is what you are after worth what it's costing you?

A few years ago, one of the credit card companies warned us that while many of us know how to spend, few of us know how to buy. The words have a modern ring to them, but they are an echo of the prophet Isaiah, who asked, "Wherefore do you spend your money for that which is not bread, and your labor for that which satisfieth not?"

> If there were dreams to sell,
> What would you buy?

The truth is that all dreams cost the same, for they cost us our life. Every day we spend our hours to buy them, and at the end we shall have spent all the time we had. "Take what you want, and pay for it," says the Spanish proverb; and we all do, and what we take we pay for with our life. Is your dream worth what it's costing you?

An ancient visionary describes Babylon the Great as a kind of Vanity Fair and lists the goods offered for our pleasure, each commodity the stuff that dreams are made on: gods of ivory or silver or gold, poised and eager to seduce us, promising us bliss and inviting our worship. The catalogue is long and varied and chills us by mentioning that among the merchandise are human souls. Souls for sale! What the writer means is that when you buy a dream you sell yourself—your soul, that is, for your soul is just another name for your self.

Poor Faustus! Doctor of Divinity, who traded his soul for twenty-five years of power and squandered it on trivia. He used it to make fun of the Pope, to enjoy grapes out of season, and to go to bed with Helen of Troy; he saw "the face that launch'd a thousand ships, and burnt the topless towers of Ilium."

> Poor Faustus!
> To buy your dream, you sold yourself.
>
> But there were dreams to sell,
> Ill didst thou buy.

Poor Richard Rich, who wanted "position" so desperately that he lied under oath to get it and thereby brought about the death of Thomas More, a great and good man. For his lie, Master Rich was made Attorney General for Wales.

Do you remember how Sir Thomas told the wretched little man that it would profit him nothing if he gained the whole world and lost his soul; and that Wales was no compensation for so great a loss?

> Poor Richard!
> To buy your dream, you sold yourself.
>
> But there were dreams to sell,
> Ill didst thou buy.

What is it you're after?

Is it worth what it's costing you?

A third question can help us discover the nature of our ambition.

3. With what is your dream incompatible?

If your dream is in, what else is out? If it stays, what has to go? Is it compatible, for example, with friendship, or dignity, or freedom, or peace of mind?

The Fine Art of Being Imperfect

You see, one of the reasons why it is important for us to know what it is we are after is that the quality of our wanting will determine the nature of our gathering in. For what we are after becomes our basic principle, and we must not expect more than our basic principle can deliver. If that sounds difficult, then let me make it plain.

If what you are after is power, you had better forget about love; it is very difficult to be *after* both. If you put self at the center, you had better be prepared to find your outer limits there; and that can be very lonely. If you believe only in justice, and not in mercy, you'd better not make any mistakes. If you are a gossip, don't look for confidences. If you believe that life is a rat race, you mustn't hope to find any dignity in it. If your basic stance is confrontation, don't expect people to knock on your door when what they need is tenderness. If you are ruthless on the way up, you shouldn't look for sympathy on the way down. If you never forgive, you must never offend. If what you are after is security, you'd better forget about ecstasy. If your work is your life, you had better keep one eye on your relationships. If you believe that your children are your possessions, you must not look for free, spontaneous and creative spirits. If you are a materialist, don't consult us gurus about spiritual values; there is little we have to say to you, and even less that you would understand. If you believe that life is purely quantitative, you had better keep your averages up. If you spread yourself thin, you mustn't expect to go deep; and if you move in the fast lane, don't set your heart on anything that takes time. If you decide to live by the sword, then, by God, you had better carry one. Because life is moral; things come round; we reap what we sow; the chickens come home to roost; fearful symmetry is the shape of life; and we really can't have it all.

If having it all is impossible, then wanting it all is incompatible with peace of mind and serenity of heart. Says Thomas à Kempis, "The humble in spirit shall dwell in a multitude of peace." But for competitive spirits who want it all, there is no peace. For them, enough is never enough, so that contentment forever eludes them. Epicurus was right: "Nothing is enough for the man for whom enough is too little."

How refreshing it is, then, to exchange the confusion of Vanity Fair and the strident cries of its vendors for the serenity of the Delectable Mountains and the simplicity of Bunyan's shepherd boy:

> I am content with what I have,
> Little be it or much;
> And Lord, contentment still I crave,
> Because Thou savest such.

Pilgrim's judgment of the lad is true: "This shepherd boy lives a merrier life and wears more of that herb called heartsease in his bosom than he that is clad in silk and velvet."

What is it you're after?

Is what you're after worth what it is costing you?

With what is your dream incompatible?

One question remains as we seek to measure our ambition.

4. Does your dream carry its own reward?

The rewards we seek range from the sublime to the despicable, some being sordid enough to betray the good things we do to get them; take the man who prayed for humility, making sure enough people saw and heard him to satisfy his pride! Now, prayer bestows many rewards, but pride ought not to be one of them. Of such people Jesus said sadly, "They have their reward." His words mean that such people are fully paid up; there is nothing left for them; they have received all there is to be had.

Some rewards, like wages, are given in return for our effort to earn them. Such recompense is honorable, being honest pay for honest work. The only problem is that we hope for more; and what we hope for is the best reward of all—that our work itself should be rewarding.

Years ago, I promised a little girl five dollars if she would learn to play the first movement of Beethoven's *Moonlight Sonata.* She learned it, and I paid up. She quickly spent the money, but she kept the sonata. She has kept it all her life. Nothing can take it away from her. Her real reward was not the money, but the music: nothing paid out at the end, but something taken in all along.

Consider the lawyer who works, not for prestige, but for justice; the physician who practices, not for profit, but for healing; the artist who creates, not for fame, but for beauty; the mother who is devoted, not for gratitude, but for love; or the saint who is good, not for reputation, but for love of goodness.

Now, when people of faith speak of the reward of heaven, those critical of faith sometimes complain that believers are a mercenary lot and that the promise of heaven is nothing more than a bribe to make people religious and keep them faithful.

Such critics fail to understand that some rewards are not only honorable, but inevitable. Heaven is not a bribe to make or keep us good; it is the home of goodness itself. It is not a payment for walking with God; it is where the road leads. It is not anything added to faith or love or beauty or truth; it is their fulfillment. It is singing the music we have learned, speaking the language we have studied, praising the mercy that has been the companion of our pilgrimage. In this sense, the reward of heaven is bestowed only on those who have carried it with them.

Such reward is fulfillment.

And such fulfillment is joy.

And joy is the business of heaven.

15

ISN'T IT ROMANTIC?

Have you any use for heroes?

The saying, "No man is a hero to his valet," comes to us from the seventeenth century, but there is a strong hint of it a thousand years earlier.

Whatever its date of origin, the statement must seem hardly worth a mention nowadays, when so few are heroic, and the heroic few are unlikely to employ the services of a valet.

Yet the words are kept alive by a question they raise and by those who have tried to answer it: If heroes are not heroes to their valets, is it because no men are heroes or because all valets are valets? That good question has ricocheted off Hegel, Goethe, Thomas Carlyle, George F. Will, and Gertrude Himmelfarb before reaching you and me.

We might wish to update it by wondering if there really are no longer any persons of true greatness and high-mindedness; or if they still exist, but are given short shrift by those journalists, historians, biographers, critics, and commentators who suffer from what someone has called "a presumption against greatness"—who have no time for heroes and take pleasure in cutting them down to their own puny size.

One wonders, for example, what sort of hero could survive the cynicism of an invasive and predatory press, the self-appointed secret police of our democracy, which unctuously presumes that the public's right to know confers an unlimited right to tell and elevates snooping to the status of a holy cause. The press sanctimoniously attempts to convince us that in depriving us of our privacy it is thinking only of our good.

When Mr. and Mrs. Bill Cosby chose to meet quietly with their family members and close friends to celebrate the life and mourn the death of their murdered son, the front-page headline in *The New York Post* read "Secret Rites for Cosby's Son."

Those interviewers, critics, and commentators who are famous only for being famous, and whose chief work is to open the door as the truly great come in and go out, often have an air of superiority and condescension about them. Without embarrassment they list the limitations of Shakespeare, or a composer's or performer's failure in this sonata or that concerto, or a football coach's foolishness in kicking instead of keeping. Why, we are told by hockey experts, who have cooled their drinks with more ice than they ever skated on, that if Wayne Gretzky would only take their advice and pass instead of shooting, or shoot instead of passing, he would be a better player.

Historians and biographers may be among the worst offenders. Familiarity with their subjects' physical, intellectual, and ethical shortcomings may entice writers of history or biography into taking the moral high ground and encourage them to reckon themselves more heroic than the heroes they diminish. They think it impossible to be both imperfect and eminent. They are certain that having feet of clay weakens the brain, atrophies the imagination, and spoils genius. If the character is flawed, the character's work cannot be any good.

Gertrude Himmelfarb likes the way in which one historian, G. R. Elton, turns the tables on cynicism and revisionism of this sort. Elton says that when he meets a historian who does not think that Winston Churchill was a great man, he knows he is not in the presence of a great historian.

The high priestess of this unhappy breed is surely Tennyson's Vivien, whose tongue, we are told, raged like a fire among the

Knights of King Arthur until she left "Not even Lancelot brave, nor Galahad clean."

The trouble is that heroism not only consists of the brave and noble ones we admire; it also constitutes a region of the human spirit. To kill our heroes is not only to commit murder, but to be guilty of suicide; it is to cast away the hero in our soul. When we have lost the power to feel the pang of valor, the thrill of fortitude, the lure of adventure, the charm of honor, the appeal of sacrifice, we shall have heard death; we shall have lived too long.

Russell Kirk once said that among the principal themes that have inspired our chief works of imaginative literature are the triumph of duty, honor, and fortitude we have mentioned, and the love that is the devotion of a truly human person to a truly human person. In this way he described and celebrated, not only the heroic, but also the romantic.

Kirk's words were precisely chosen. They remind us that "doing what comes naturally" is not an excuse for acting like animals, but an invitation to behave humanly by expressing the love of one truly human person for another truly human person.

We used to speak of making love; now we talk of having sex. But they are not the same; and it is not the puritan in me, but the romantic, that wishes to preserve the difference and deplores the way the wind is blowing.

Sex is merely a function we share with the beasts. Having sex may be just one more way of indulging our selfishness. Somebody said once that when a young man whispers, "I love you," he may really mean, "I love me and I want you." But listen to what it *can* mean: "So Jacob served seven years for Rachel, and they seemed to him but a few days because of the love he had for her."

To make love is to humanize an animal appetite by making it the expression of friendship, respect, devotion, restraint, and faithfulness. If you think that making love in this way will diminish your pleasure or spoil your ecstasy, you have forgotten

The Fine Art of Being Imperfect

that most of the world's great love poetry was written by men and women who believed what I have said. Read, young lovers, the words of Henry James in "The Wings of a Dove":

> He went on with that fantasy, but at this point Kate ceased to attend. He saw after a little that she had been following some thought of her own. Suddenly she said to him with extraordinary beauty: "I engage myself to you for ever . . . and I pledge you—I call God to witness!—every spark of my faith; I give you every drop of my life." That was all, for the moment, but it was enough, and it was almost as quiet as if it were nothing. They moved by a common instinct to a spot, within sight, that struck them as fairly sequestered, and there, before their time together was spent . . . they had exchanged vows and tokens, sealed their rich compact, solemnized, so far as breathed words and murmured sounds, and lighted eyes and clasped hands could do it, their agreement to belong only, and to belong tremendously to each other.

I was astonished, bewildered, and disappointed to learn that some of our major universities have decided to offer courses in English literature without teaching Shakespeare. Have they found a better dramatist to study? How perverse that our young people, who pay good money to meet the best that has been thought and written, will not be formally introduced to Lady Macbeth, Sir John Falstaff, Prospero, the Moor of Venice, Lear, Cordelia, the Prince of Denmark, Richard III, and Henry V.

The deprivation is more grievous even than this, though; for the man who told us that "all the world's a stage, and all the men and women merely players" stood a pretty fair chance of getting them to see their own life as drama. If he had managed to do that, he would have given them not only a truth to see, but a way of seeing.

One of Malcolm Muggeridge's favorite sayings was, "Life is a drama, not a process." With these words, Muggeridge invited us to interpret life, not in the vocabulary or by the categories of the sciences, hard or soft, but in language that is personal, individual, and dramatic. He distrusted nouns such as "progress" and adjectives such as "evolving," with their suggestion of inevitable, irresistible betterment. He was skeptical of the whole idea of progress and he once had a public, mischievous, and spirited debate with Bertrand Russell on the subject. He would have agreed with Ogden Nash that "progress was a good idea once but has been going on too long."

When I was a theological student, I was told that God's revelation of Himself in Scripture was a "progressive" revelation. It sounded all of a piece with Émile Coué's, "Every day, in every way, I'm getting better and better," except that the revelation wouldn't have budged an inch without the dominant characters in Israel's history. The advance was not a movement of the masses, who usually resisted it; it was the work of inspired individuals of extraordinary clarity, character, conscience, compassion, and courage, who suffered for it. Moses led it, and Elijah, and Ruth, and Job, and Amos, and Hosea, and Jeremiah.

This is a useful thing to remember in these days when the importance both of heroes and villains is diminished in favor of the common people; when movements are alleged to be more important than those who move them; when we have revolutions, but not revolutionaries; reform, but not reformers; tyrannies, but not tyrants. History thus becomes faceless, shaped by Fascism without Mussolini, Nazism without Hitler, and Communism without Stalin.

This is not only strange, but dangerous stuff for democracy. It reminds me that in *Brave New World,* the two books that must be kept under lock and key are the Bible and *The Works of William Shakespeare.* Huxley's dystopia of depleted personalities would not have survived exposure to the transcendently good or tragically evil characters to be found in these works. Once they had read such literature, who could any longer be content with anonymity!

The Fine Art of Being Imperfect

We seek the dramatic everywhere but in ourselves. We look for the tension of it in our music, movies, plays, sports, and politics. We love the game that goes into sudden-death overtime, the fighter who snatches victory from defeat, the politician who snatches defeat from victory. We hold our breath as Othello disintegrates before our eyes.

Yet the drama is not only the hero's, but ours; for the hero's soul is not more precious than our own. The heroic, the romantic, the dramatic are not only the elements that make a great play or a noble action or a transcendent symphony; they are the stuff of character; they are what makes us genuinely human.

16

BELIEVING AND SEEING

Do you believe what you see, or see what you believe?

The common saying, "Seeing is believing," is well on its way to becoming a popular proverb, rather like "Look before you leap" or "Many hands make light work."

"Seeing is believing" not only makes a statement, though; it also expresses an attitude, adopts a stance. It even makes a demand, for if seeing is believing, then "show me!"

The phrase sometimes expresses the skepticism toward religious belief of those who regard the devout as a self-deceived, credulous lot who allow themselves to be persuaded by the flimsiest evidence, so long as it serves to strengthen their convictions and confirm their prejudices.

Now, some belief is like that—not only credulous, but superstitious. Some religious hope is little better than wishful thinking, and some faith is almost indistinguishable from magic. But those who believe only what they see go too far the other way, for their attitude will shut them out of some of the most profound human experiences and enterprises.

To begin with, believing only what we see won't work in business. Not only will it fail to make a successful entrepreneur, it will strangle any business that already exists.

Not long ago, the author of a book on the history of Pan American Airlines, which no longer exists but was once among the most successful airlines in the world, explained its rise and fall by saying that Pan Am was born in a vision and perished for

106

lack of one. But a vision is not something we catch with our eye, it is a way of seeing. Like light, vision is invisible to sight but enables us to see everything else.

Several years ago, I understood a task both promising and hazardous. One man who could have helped immensely said to me, "Show me it won't fail, and I'll support you." I told him that by the time I could show him it wouldn't fail I wouldn't need his support. He was like the third-rate bank manager who will lend us all the money we need so long as we can prove we don't need it.

No great business enterprise, no commercial empire, no noble city, nation, or civilization was ever built, sustained, or elevated by those who see only what is. Everything is built by those who dream what never was but might yet be. Yet if we speak of this to those who believe only what they see, they will not understand what we are talking about. Not only so; their attitude will put a drag on our action, crush our initiative, and wither our hopes.

Our own great nation was a vision long before it was a republic—a hope and a longing before it became a reality. America is an idea great enough to become an ideal, an ideal great enough to be unattainable. That is why the very idea of America is infused with great spiritual and transcendent power. The ideal of America is forever within our grasp and forever beyond our reach. Ideals easily attainable cease even to be interesting.

Our "seeing is believing" persons will fare no better among creative artists. If they declare that they will believe only what they see, the creative artists will reply that in their art there isn't anything to see. All the writers, composers, painters, and sculptors in the world declare that their hope is to bring into being something that was not there before. No one will ever see it, read it, sing it, hear it, or play it until they make it. That is what it means to create. In this sense, the artist's work is done by faith, not by sight; and that faith is the very condition of creativity.

Indeed, the best artists go even further and tell us that they not only seek to create, but are sometimes astonished by their creation. As Robert Frost remarked, "No surprise for the writer, no surprise for the reader!" Sometimes an artist's words, music, or characters take on a life of their own so that the artist's work is one not merely of expression, but of discovery. Ernest Hemingway told Robert Manning, editor of *The Atlantic,* that when he wrote *The Old Man and the Sea,* he did not know whether or not the great fish was going to bite when it began to circle and started to smell the old fisherman's bait. Hemingway had to write on, "inventing out of knowledge," as he put it. Flannery O'Connor said that when she began writing she did not know how her story "Good Country People" would end. She had to discover how it would end. The poet C. Day Lewis used to say that poetry is not merely the expression of truth in verse, but the discovery of truth in verse.

These are some of the reasons why totalitarian regimes have always been threatened by, and therefore sought to control, their writers, painters, and composers. Every great writer is a kind of second government, and the visions and dreams of poets and musicians have disturbed the slumber of tyrants. Arthur O'Shaughnessey speaks for all creative artists when he tells us:

> We are the music-makers,
> And we are the dreamers of dreams. . . .

The deepest need of those who have no vision is the need to catch the spirit of that solitary dreamer on whose soul has broken a light that does not depart, and who can turn the hearts of others to fire.

Those for whom seeing is believing will not be any more at home among the scientists than they were among the artists and businessmen, for it is the scientists who warn us that if we believe only what we see—or indeed, if we believe what we see—our

The Fine Art of Being Imperfect

eyes will deceive us, and our beliefs will be mistaken. They agree with Blake that:

> We ever must believe a lie
> When we see *with*, not *through*, the eye.

They know that what is needed to believe truly is not only sight but insight, not only perception but perceptiveness. They go on to astonish us by saying fantastic things: that light is subject to gravity, that matter is really energy, and that no one has ever seen, heard, or touched the protons, neutrons, and electrons of which matter is made. We know they exist, not because we've ever observed them, but because they can be held in a meaningful and useful pattern that is itself a mental concept.

All this is to say that scientists do their best work not only by the accuracy of their observations, but by the fertility of their imagination. They begin and proceed, not only by looking, but also by wondering. They properly belong among the artists and philosophers. They become wise, not by things seen and heard, but by things understood.

But the most crippling inadequacy of the "seeing is believing" attitude is its failure to understand the energy, and grasp the subtlety, of human relationships.

When Jack falls in love with Jill, the old gossips are likely to mutter over their coffee cups, "I don't know what he sees in her," or "I don't know what she sees in him." They are exactly right. They don't know. But Jack and Jill know. He finds in his beloved the fulfillment of all his dreams of loveliness; and she, looking at him, thinks there is nobody like him in the world.

Now, who comes closer to the truth in this, the old gossips or the young lovers? You may remember that William James answered the question by siding with Jack and Jill. His reason was that love, trust, and sympathy reveal what suspicion, fear, and cynicism hide. If you don't trust me, you will never know me, for I won't let you see anything I care about.

Of course there is a place for caution and suspicion in our dealings with others, but it is not first place. It is secondary. When we meet those who are suspicious of everyone, we do not praise their astuteness, we suggest a therapist.

One of our worst lies is that love is blind. We know that it isn't, for it has sometimes discovered in us more than we could ever have found in ourselves. Love has loved us into loving and smiled us into smiling and saved us from inferiority, self-hatred, and despair. We are not loved because we are worthy; we are worthy because we are loved. This may be said of all true love, both human and Divine. As the old hymn by Frederick Faber put it:

> That Thou should'st think
> so much of me
> And be the God Thou art,
> Is darkness to my intellect,
> But sunshine to my heart!

I began by saying that the phrase "Seeing is believing" is close to acceptance as a popular proverb. Now, I notice that the best proverbs contradict each other. "Look before you leap," we say; but then, "He who hesitates is lost." Many hands do make light work, but we know that too many cooks can spoil the broth. "Faint heart never won fair lady," we tell the timid; but we warn the impetuous that to marry in haste is to repent at leisure. It seems that every proverb not only affirms its own truth but also keeps another proverb honest.

How are we to contain and balance "Seeing is believing"? I think by putting it into reverse and saying that believing is seeing—that faith shows us a reality not visible to the naked eye.

Years ago I drove sixty miles to the cinema, but I noticed when I got there that the picture on the screen was out of focus. Ava

The Fine Art of Being Imperfect

Gardner was blurred around the edges. I complained to the attendant, who mentioned it to the manager, who told the projectionist, who tried to fix it. But the projectionist didn't improve it much. Then driving home, I noticed that the highway signs were out of focus, and there was no one to complain to. So I had my eyes tested, and I was astonished to discover how much I had been missing.

We must not say that love is blind, and we must not speak of blind faith; for faith, like love, is a way of seeing. It is like wearing glasses that bring into focus what is there, ready and waiting to be seen, when the eyes of our eyes are opened. Augustine wrote:

> To have faith is to believe what you cannot see,
> And the reward of faith is to see what you believe.

The trouble with those who won't move beyond "Seeing is believing" is that they don't believe enough to see, and therefore cannot see enough to believe.

17
WILDERNESS EXPERIENCES

Would you choose comfort over character?

The Wilderness Act of 1964 declares, "A wilderness is hereby recognized as an area where the earth and its community of life are untrammeled by man, where man himself is a visitor who does not remain."

I first read those words in the window of a New York shoe store that offered for sale a wide selection of hiking boots. The suggestion was, I suppose, that the boots were good enough, not only to comfortably carry us in, but also to safely bear us out of those wilderness places where we are visitors who do not remain. I wondered at the time if the lawyer who framed the Wilderness Act was Jewish, for one of the meanings of the Hebrew word for wilderness is "a place you pass through."

Notice, to begin with, that we can turn any region of the world's land, sea, or sky into a wilderness by the manner of our passing through it. We can do it, for example, by our overreaching; by making ourselves lords of creation when the Creator intended that we should be stewards of creation; by forgetting that the world was not given to us, but is entrusted to us. The very word "stewardship" is a gift from religious faith to those who seek to protect the earth from the pillaging of its resources.

Others make the world a wilderness by passing through it too quickly. We boast of our ability to annihilate distance, forgetting that if we drive in the fast lane we won't have time to attend to anything. Let me ask you: How far is a mile?

One answer is that a mile is a minute. All miles are minutes when we drive at sixty miles an hour. But when I was a boy a mile took me past the tree stump, and over the stream where the watercress grew and trout hid in the shadows. It passed the old mill and the two horses, one black the other white, that trotted over to be fed sycamore leaves. A mile in those days was not a minute. It was an afternoon of adventure and enchantment.

Now, when we pass blindly over the earth we not only make the world a wilderness, we kill the poetry that is the deepest part of us. Thomas Hardy said that he wished to be remembered as "a poet who noticed things." Of course! For things are there to be noticed, and it is the work of poets to notice them. But how are we to notice anything if we have no time to stand and stare?

Some forms of religious faith have made the world a wilderness by their suspicion of beauty and pleasure and their enmity to joy. In Ibsen's *Emperor and Galilean*, the Emperor asks:

> Have you looked at these Christians closely? Hollow-eyed, pale-cheeked, flat-breasted all. The sun shines for them but they do not see it. The earth offers them its fullness, but they desire it not. All their desire is to renounce and suffer that they may come to die.

Swinburne's complaint against Jesus of Nazareth was that he had drained all the color out of existence:

> Thou hast conquered, O pale Galilean,
> The world has grown gray from thy breath.

Now, some Christians may be like that, but the Galilean wasn't. And the earliest Christians knew it. In the crude art of their catacombs they depicted Him as Orpheus, whose music was such an enchantment that "the trees and the mountaintops that freeze, bow themselves when He did sing . . . even the billows of the sea hung their heads" to hear Him play, and at the sound of His lute, plants and flowers thought they dwelt in an eternal spring.

When I was a child, I used to hear the grown-ups sing:

> Earth is but a desert drear,
> Heaven is my home.

They sang it heartily; but I never believed them. How could I, when I lived every day with my eyes out on my cheeks in astonishment, and my heart filled with wonder in a world of wonders! Heaven was my true home, but in those days I could, like Blake

> . . . see a world in a grain of sand,
> And a heaven in a wildflower,
> Hold infinity in the palm of my hand
> And eternity in an hour.

Religion at its best has always been life-affirming, not life-denying. True faith is an echo of God's "Yes" to His Creation, when He pronounced it "very good," and "the morning stars sang together, and all the sons of God shouted for joy" on the first day of the world. Some pleasures may be evil, but it is not the pleasure that makes them so. On the Day of Judgment we shall be called to account, not only for those sins we have committed, but for those good gifts of God that we have not enjoyed.

The word "wilderness" describes not only a geographical location, an area of the earth's surface, but also a region of the human spirit and a dimension of human experience. We have "wilderness experiences," not only by hiking in desert places, but also when some life-shattering disappointment or sorrow or illness or rejection or failure scatters all sense of meaning and

The Fine Art of Being Imperfect

leaves us abandoned in an appalling solitariness. In this waste-land the springs of joy have dried up, and the rivers of hope that once rushed in full flood have become a bed of cracked and burning clay, and there is no help for us in a parched and desolate place.

Now, the heartening thing to notice is that the word "wilder-ness," which so aptly describes our predicament, is also the hint and promise of our deliverance. For if a wilderness is a place we pass through, then wilderness experiences will pass. They are not final descriptions of anything. They are not full stops and dead ends, but parentheses, incidents of the journey, accidents of our pilgrimage, happenings on the way.

W. B. Yeats once said that the most terrible thing about the miseries of childhood is that to the child they appear endless. But adults know better. We have what Nathaniel Hawthorne once called "the greatest of all mortal consolations," the knowledge that "this too will pass." And so we wait. And such waiting is not a passive resignation, but a lively expectation.

Once, when I asked a friend, "how are you?" she replied, "I'm waiting." For years she had known periods of depression. She also knew, from experience, that with the help of a wise physi-cian, the love of her family, and the support of her friends, the depression would pass. It was with a sense of sureness that she said, "I'm waiting." Her waiting was the expression of hope, her denial of despair. She was confident that, in the word's of Browning's "Paracelsus,"

> If I stoop into a dark tremendous sea of cloud
>   It is but for a time.
> I hold God's lamp close to my breast.
> Its splendor soon or late will pierce the gloom.
>   I shall emerge one day.

Please notice that such waiting is a kind of doing. Sometimes it is success of a sort just to get the days in without giving up. We must not be disappointed that our victory does not make us feel splendidly heroic or gladly triumphant. Often it takes all the energy, faith, and fortitude we have just to win through to nightfall. We are like a boxer who has been hit with a heavy punch; all he can do is hang on until the end of the round. There is little glory in hanging on, and not much dignity either; but then it is not a matter of glory, but of survival.

The hopefulness of such waiting makes patience a quality we possess, not a helplessness that others impose on us. We know what it is like when we board an aircraft and it pulls back from the gate in good time: we naively imagine we are on our way. Not so! Our favorite airline is merely setting us up so that it can thank us for our patience. Because when it seems that we are within striking distance of the runway, the captain announces that we are two hundred and seventy-fourth in the line of aircraft waiting to take to the air. He regrets the delay. Then come the words that signal the death of hope: "Thank you for your patience."

There I sit, strapped in an aluminum tube, with no prospect of catching my connecting flight, being told not only cheerily, but chirpily, by a total stranger who has never met me and may wish me no good, that he is grateful for the patience I don't have. No wonder one philosopher defined patience as "despair disguised as virtue." Patience is no longer a quality we possess, but something people do to us.

Some time ago, I watched a fight on television, not as you might suppose, between two hockey players, but between two professional pugilists who were good at their job. Gil Clancy, who knows about boxing, said that one of them was a world-class fighter because he was patient. A patient fighter! Nothing passive about that! What is it that makes a fighter patient? I think I know, because I know nearly as much about boxing as Gil Clancy. First, a patient fighter is there for the whole contest. Whether the fight lasts eight, ten, or twelve rounds, he's ready to go the distance.

Next, he believes that he has enough time to do what he has to do. Third, he respects his opponent and does not underestimate him. Finally, he has a sureness that he can outlast the other man, and win.

Now, that sort of patience is not disguised despair, it is a positive achievement. It is power. It has about it what someone once called "a soft invincibility," which is the promise of victory.

The psalmist knew this quality of waiting, this "soft invincibility," but found it, not in himself, but in God. He was patient because he was trustful—confident because he waited for the Eternal. Listen to his words:

> I waited patiently for the LORD;
>   He inclined to me and heard my cry.
> Happy are those who make the LORD their trust.

A wilderness is a place we pass through, but passing experiences may yield lasting benefits. This is especially true of wilderness experiences. We pass through them, but the person who comes out is not the person who went in. I think that's why we like to talk about the hard times we have come through. Most of us are like the old sailor who said, "I don't like being in a storm at sea, but I like having been in a storm at sea."

Now, it's not hard to understand why wilderness experiences yield enduring qualities, for most of the qualities we covet can be gained only in difficult circumstances. There is no such thing as easy courage, for example. Courage is always difficult. If it's easy, it isn't courage. To be courageous, we have to be afraid. Being courageous does not mean that we are not afraid; it means that we are afraid, but we refuse to allow our fears to determine our actions. And that's hard. Only courage can do it!

We must be careful not to wish for qualities without some awareness of their cost. Hemingway once defined fortitude as grace under pressure, which is a way of telling us that if we want fortitude, we'd better get ready for pressure. We shall never discover the meaning of hope until we have come close to despair, or of freedom until our liberty is threatened. If we wish to be brave, we can no longer enjoy self-pity. We can't be forgiving without having something to forgive, and that will not be easy; for what we have to forgive may have wounded our spirit and broken our heart. If we wish to stand alone, we must surrender our need to be affirmed and our dependence on the approval of others. If we long for integrity, we'd better learn how to say no and where to draw a line. If we wish to be sympathetic, we shall not be able to keep the suffering of others at a distance.

I read of a man who grew impatient with his own impatience and asked God to help him. Next morning, he missed his train. He didn't think much of that answer; but it is the only kind of answer that is possible. We can learn patience only in circumstances that invite our impatience. We must be careful about what we ask for. We might just get it, and the quality we covet may cost us more than we expect or are willing to pay.

Everything depends on whether we believe our character to be more important than our comfort. I have no doubt at all that God thinks it is. That is why He denies us peace that He may give us glory, and why the only rest He offers us is in that Peace which created the world.

18

PILGRIMS ALL

If you're not a pilgrim, what are you?

Some years ago James Pike, Episcopal Bishop of New York, parked his car at the side of the road that runs through the Judean wilderness and with his wife, stepped into the desert to explore it. He never found his way back. Bishop Pike perished in the wilderness, and his wife nearly did.

As we have seen, the Hebrew word for wilderness means a place one passes through. To stay in the wilderness is to die there. The Hebrew word was born of Hebrew experience. The tribes of Israel passed through the wilderness on their journey of escape from the tyranny of Egypt, across the River Jordan to the Land of Promise.

This means that the word describes not only the wilderness, but also the nature of those who journey through it. They are pilgrims. The desert is not their home; they do not dwell there. Their identity is symbolized, not by the firm foundations and solid stones of a temple, but by a tabernacle—a moving tent, which is struck every morning and every night is pitched a day's march nearer home.

This idea of life as pilgrimage has proved a pervasive and enduring one. Christians are indebted to Islam for a saying of Jesus not recorded in the Gospels, but preserved on the wall of a mosque near Delhi. It reads, "Jesus, on whom be peace, said, 'This world is a bridge; pass over it but do not build your dwelling there.'"

119

John Bunyan begins his *Pilgrim's Progress* with the words, "As I passed through the wilderness of this world. . . . " It was the idea of pilgrimage that informed the men and women of faith who on November 11, 1620, arrived near Cape Cod after sixty-six days at sea. They journeyed from the oppression of an established church and an old country to the liberty of a promised land and a new commonwealth. Their River Jordan was as wide as the broad Atlantic and their land of promise was the country in which you and I now dwell. William Bradford, the second governor of the Plymouth Colony, wrote of those travelers:

> What could they see but a hideous and desolate wilderness? Neither could they, as it were, go up to the mountain-top to view from this wilderness a more Godly country to feed their hopes. For which way soever they turned their eyes, save upward to the heavens, they could have little solace or content in respect of any outward objects.

Six months after their arrival, half the pilgrims were dead, including John Carver, the first governor of the colony. Yet when the *Mayflower* was ready to set sail for England, her captain offering free passage to any who wished to accompany him, no one turned back. As Governor Bradford said of them, "They knew they were pilgrims."

So also did the Black Americans who, like the children of Israel, journeyed through a wilderness in their flight from slavery to freedom. Their spirituals are full of this awareness:

> Go down Moses, way down to Egypt's land.
> Tell ole Pharaoh, "Let my people go!"
> The Lord told Moses what to do
> To lead the children of Israel through.
> "Let my people go!"

We are pilgrims all. But what does it mean to be a pilgrim?

The Fine Art of Being Imperfect

I think, to begin with, that it means we travel hopefully. Sometimes the pilgrim hope was otherworldly. It had to be, for there was nothing to hope for in this world. American slaves sang their "sorrow songs," as they called them, to express their despair of this world. Freedom from slavery and freedom from life were often synonymous in their thought and in their music. The only deliverance was death. All they could do was steal away to Jesus and wait for that chariot that would come to carry them home.

It was the particular genius of Martin Luther King, Jr., to show us that hope works on two levels, and that both levels are vital. There is hope for this world: that we can make something of it, and of ourselves in it. And there is hope beyond this world. The earthly and heavenly expectations are inseparable, for they gather conviction and gain validity from each other.

Martin Luther King had a dream for time and a hope for eternity. He was, at one and the same moment, constitutional and theological, political and devotional, both heavenly minded and of great earthly use, as he called us back to the very idea of America and forward to the City of God.

He knew he was a pilgrim; and it was in the hopefulness of pilgrimage that he found his courage. He told us so himself, when, anticipating his own violent and untimely death, he said he was not afraid, for he had passed through the wilderness, had been to the mountaintop, had seen Beulah Land and caught a glimpse of the glory to which he traveled.

A second characteristic of pilgrims is that they know wilderness experiences are to be passed through. To dwell in them is to perish in them. Yet many of us choose to stay in a desert of guilt or addiction or inferiority or destructive relationships or grief or cynicism or grievance, when we should have passed through them long ago.

Sometimes our best hope of passing through is to seek the help of others: a wise physician, a skilled therapist, a spiritual counselor, a trusted friend, a community of fellow travelers who share a common predicament and are banded together for mutual encouragement. Sometimes we are perfectly capable of emerging on our own, by allowing a new insight to create a new attitude. But it's not easy.

We all know people who don't merely have complaints, but have become complaints. They have so dwelt in their petulance that their petulance has taken them over. They would lose their identity if they were to surrender their sense of grievance and their right to be miserable. Others wouldn't know who they were if they didn't see themselves as victims. They find it easier to blame others for their difficulties than to accept responsibility for their own foolish decisions and thoughtless actions.

Still others would be struck speechless if they couldn't gossip. We all find it easier to justify ourselves than to accept criticism, even when it is justified. Some of us would rather allow jealousy to consume us and see life with a jaundiced eye than discipline our imagination and learn to be trustful. We find it easier to indulge our self-pity and trade our courage for sympathy than to confront the fears that possess us. We all know men and women—we may be among them—whose grief or anger or inferiority or inordinate touchiness is not their problem, but their solution. It defines them; has become the dominant characteristic of their personality, what their friends have come to expect of them. Even when they catch a glimpse of what they are really like, they find it easier to remain where they are than to move.

Auden was right: We would sooner die than change. And because we will not change, the most heroic, loving, and generous part of us withers in the wilderness we refuse to leave. Let me say to you what I have often good reason to tell myself: If you don't change anything, nothing will change.

Yet all the time God offers us the strength of His presence. His promise is not that He will save us from our wilderness experiences, but that He will bring us through them. If He denies us peace, it is to give us glory. For we are from God and journey to God. He will give us a light to bring us to everlasting life.

Notice how our awareness that we are pilgrims explains our homesickness.

Like Bunyan's Pilgrim, I have always known that the wilderness of this world is a place to pass through, because I have never felt at home in it. This has been most true, not when I have been most unhappy, but when my appreciation of this world has ravished me and my joys have been so deep and tender as to fill me with an inconsolable longing.

When I was little, I didn't understand this and never told it. My most poignant perceptions of goodness and beauty were unshared secrets, divulged to neither parents nor friends, for truth to tell, they were beyond telling, even to myself.

Then one day I read Malcolm Muggeridge and learned that, both as child and man, he had a feeling of not being a native, of knowing himself a stranger in this world. He speaks of the inconceivable poignancy with which he first heard the phrase in the Bible, "a stranger in a stange land." It confirmed his deepest awareness of himself and told him who he was.

On another day I read C. S. Lewis, who writes of his lifelong nostalgia, his desire for his own far-off country, most present when he was most happy. It led him to ask a question and to frame an argument. His question, as he asked it in *Mere Christianity*, was, "If I am really a product of a materialistic universe, how is it that I do not feel at home here?" And his argument, sometimes called "The Argument from Desire," was, "If I find in myself a desire which no experience in this world can satisfy, the most probable explanation is that I was made for another world."

On other days I read Plato and Plotinus, Augustine and John Donne, Henry Vaughan and George Herbert, Thomas Traherne and William Wordsworth, G. K. Chesterton and W. B. Yeats, who ended my loneliness by telling me that they had known for centuries what I had so lately discovered: that an unattainable ecstasy waits just beyond the grasp of our consciousness. That our best havings are wantings, and that the truest clue to our nature is our longing.

Sometimes I am asked if I believe in heaven. I not only believe in it, I long for it, and I know what it will be like from all the hints, intimations, and promises that have reached me as I have passed through the wilderness of this world. All beauty here has spoken to me of "the Beauty Yonder." Here we are but strangers and pilgrims. In the Land of Promise, in the Country of the Great King, we shall be at home.

The Fine Art of Being Imperfect

19

ON BEING CONTENT

*Have you learned to distinguish between
your circumstances and your environment?*

When the Apostle Paul told his friends at Philippi that he was content, they knew him well enough to understand that he did not mean by this any of the things that have given contentment a bad name.

He was not smug, complacent, or self-satisfied. He had neither lost his zeal nor surrendered his vision. His life was not lacking in drama, tension, or anxiety. And his friends knew that his serenity did not depend on favorable circumstances, but that he had learned to be content whatever his circumstances.

The Stoic philosophers had a word for all this, and Paul did not hesitate to use it. The word had become almost a technical term of Stoicism to describe a contentment that was not passive but active: an overcoming of adversity and mastery of circumstances achieved by discipline of mind and refinement of spirit. It was not something that happened to them but something they made happen. The Stoic ideal was to be a thermostat that controlled the temperature, not a thermometer that merely registered it.

To achieve this, the Stoics amassed much practical wisdom, gathered from experience, refined in practice, and often expressed in aphorisms easily remembered and readily assimilated. The followers of Epictetus, for example, wrote down enough of their master's sayings to fill a book. Epictetus was a slave, who limped from a wound inflicted by a vicious master. He came along a little later than Paul, but his instruction includes much of the teaching that enabled Paul to be content.

Epictetus tells us that before we become attached to anything beautiful we should ask ourselves, "What is its nature?" A glass vase, for example, may be pretty enough to win our admiration, but we should remember that it is not only bright but brittle. Set it on a shelf, and it will delight us for a lifetime. Drop it, and its beauty will be shattered in an instant and lost forever.

In other words, we should be reconciled to the nature of things and allow their nature to determine our actions and inform our expectations. If we fail to do so, we shall be disappointed, bewildered, and resentful. When Margaret Fuller, the New England Transcendentalist, remarked that she "accepted the universe," Thomas Carlyle exclaimed, "By God, she'd better!" I heard of a patient who complained to his physician that he didn't like the night air, and received the matter-of-fact reply that during certain hours of the twenty-four, night air is the only air there is.

This is what George MacDonald called "the factitude of things." Facts should be regarded as occupying space. There is no getting around, over, or under them. They are simply there, and they will not alter their nature to suit our whims. Wishing does not make it so. Water will certainly wet, and fire will surely burn, and during certain hours of the twenty-four, night air is the only air there is.

This "factitude of things" should be allowed not only to instruct our minds but also to inform our expectations. C. S. Lewis once said that the world is like a building. Half the people who live in it think it a prison, while the other half think it a five-star hotel. Those who think it a prison can't get over how good things are, while those who think it a hotel are always complaining about the room service.

But what kind of building is the world? If we believe it has been designed for our comfort and security we shall expect certain luxuries, come to regard them as our right, and be not only disappointed but offended if we don't get them. If, by contrast, we see the world as "a vale of soul-making" we shall not be surprised when we encounter adversity. We'll know that adversity comes with the territory. Nor shall we complain when God seems careless of our comfort for the sake of our character and denies us peace to give us glory.

But the Stoics went even further, not only to consider the nature of things, but also to consider the nature of their own nature, and what they should expect of it. Being human, how should we behave?

They answered their question quaintly: Just as there are garments that suit the body, so there is behavior that suits the soul: a way of being that fits our nature as rational creatures, a way of acting that is becoming to us. This means, of course, that some conduct is unbecoming; it doesn't suit our nature at all.

Have you ever noticed, for example, how unnatural a lie is? As Sir Walter Scott knew, telling a lie is so unnatural that we cannot be competent liars without possessing an excellent memory:

> Oh, what a tangled web we weave
> When first we practice to deceive!

Truth is not like that. It is natural and spontaneous. We don't need to rehearse it or scrutinize it to remember what we said last time. We may be caught in a lie, but we cannot be caught in a truth. Honesty suits our nature and expresses it with purity of heart, clarity of thought, and directness of speech. As Orwell used to say, "Nothing helps a good style like sincerity." Epictetus puts this beautifully:

> What else can I do, a lame old man, than sing hymns to God? If I were a nightingale, I would play the part of a nightingale. But I am a rational creature; and I ought to praise God. This is my work. I do

it; nor will I desert this post so long as I am allowed to keep it. And
I exhort you to join in the same song.

Before you become attached to anything, ask yourself, "What is
its nature?"

Here is another of Epictetus's aphorisms: "Everything has two
handles; by one you can carry it, by the other, you can't."

Once again, he gives us an example. Suppose your brother has
offended you. You may attempt to carry the estrangement by the
handle of the injury. If you do, your brooding on the offense can
only make it more bitter. But you may decide to carry the
estrangement, not by the handle of the offense, but by the handle
of the relationship: My brother may have offended me; nevertheless he is my brother! If you allow your thought to dwell on that,
you may yet be reconciled to your brother.

Before we do anything we should consider what we wish to
accomplish and adapt our means to our goal. Power is the ability
to achieve purpose.

We are sometimes tempted to describe as "powerful" what is
merely loud and forceful. Yet some things that are full of sound
and fury really do signify nothing. For all the noise they make
and energy they expend, they do not accomplish their purpose.
And we sometimes describe as "weak" what is patient, gentle,
and restrained. These qualities don't make much noise; they are
not assertive or overwhelming; yet they often fulfill our intention. They are not to be regarded as weakness if they do what we
wish them to do. To employ them wisely is to suit our actions to
our purpose and carry our purpose by the right handle.

Here is a father whose daughter insists on keeping company
with a young man of whom the father does not approve. What is
he to do about it? I know fathers who have put on a show of
parental authority and outrage. They have thrown the furniture
about, frightening the family members and terrifying the family
pets: "Don't you see that young man again!" they have roared.

The Fine Art of Being Imperfect

It sounds enormously impressive and looks overwhelmingly powerful; yet I have never seen it accomplish what the father wished it to accomplish. It has usually done the opposite, driving the young lady into the young man's arms—and sometimes into his apartment. A wiser parent might remember, not only that he doesn't like the young man, but also that the young woman is his daughter. Then he would seek to sustain his relationship with her by patience, tenderness, and respect. In this way he would remain his daughter's good friend and be of some use to her in making her own responsible, mature, and loving decision.

When this does not happen, it can be inexpressibly sad and the cause of much anguish. I know one father who acted so rashly and so angrily that he lost the little girl he loved. When he resisted her marriage to the man she adored, she went away and never returned.

Be reconciled to the nature of things.

Carry them by the right handle.

In a third aphorism, Epictetus tells us that "the ignorant man never looks to himself, but to the world outside, for benefit or harm. The wise man, however, always looks to himself for benefit or harm."

Everytime I hear these words of Epictetus, they remind me of the difference between circumstances and environment. Circumstances, "the world outside," are often "given." There's not much we can do about them. Yet we are not entirely helpless, because from our circumstances we may choose our environment, select those elements we will allow to influence our moods and determine our attitudes.

New Yorkers do it all the time. In the subway they lose themselves in *The New York Times*, or a textbook, or novel. On Fifth Avenue they shut out the sounds of midtown Manhattan and listen to Brahms or Sibelius on their headphones. Or they enter their own inner world of beauty and enchantment.

I know an American novelist from West Virginia who was almost deaf and was told that soon she would be blind. Her reply was, "Not to worry! If the world be closed without, I'll sail the hidden seas within." Her hidden seas were like the great oceans of the world: broad, and deep, and beautiful, and teeming with life.

I know a man who will never lose *Paradise Lost,* for he has learned it by heart. Another has done the same thing with Shakespeare's historical plays, and yet another with *Pilgrim's Progress.* I know two physicians who meet regularly to exchange sonnets they have learned by heart.

One young lady confessed, "Deep down, I'm shallow." But there are others who, deep down, are deep. And their depth sustains them. They are strengthened and protected by their rich interior life. E. M. Forster once described Matthew Arnold's poetry as "a garden of enchantment" and went on to say that its beauty is not mere gossamer, but part of our "outfit against brutality."

Years ago, I read of a young woman afflicted with polio. When someone remarked that her paralysis would color her life, she replied that it would, but that she would choose the color. Think of the colors: green for envy, yellow for self-pity, blue for depression, red for rage, black for despair. She chose the silver of hope and the gold of courage and found benefit in herself, not harm from the world outside.

Such contentment is the work of fortitude and the gift of grace. It reminds us that every life may be *Ein Heldenleben*, "A Hero's Life": not ideal, but noble; not complete, but hopeful; not perfect, but faithful, beautiful, and good.

20

YOUR PLACE OF POWER

How are you in your place of power?

The trouble with power is that the only people who love it are those who have it. The rest fear it, distrust it, seek to limit it, and frequently hate it.

The universal misuse of power has bred a universal suspicion of it. Lord Acton, in a letter to Bishop Creighton, warned that "power tends to corrupt, and absolute power corrupts absolutely." Consequently, "a nation must never abandon its fate to an authority it cannot control."

That is why we have democracy and elections. There are those who believe in democracy because they imagine we are all so good that each of us deserves a vote. A better reason to believe in democracy is that we are all so bad that none of us can be trusted with much power for very long.

Democracy enables us to have elections, whose primary purpose is, not to put people in, but to throw people out. When Mary rejoices, in the words of the Magnificat, so beloved of Christians in Advent season, that God "has shown strength with his arm; He has scattered the proud in the thoughts of their hearts. He has brought down the powerful from their thrones, and lifted up the lowly," we may surely be forgiven some mental reservation. We know that the humble quickly become the proud while the meek swiftly learn all the tricks and appropriate all the perks of the mighty and must therefore, in their turn, be chucked down.

Lenin believed that the vital question about power is always, "Who, whom?" meaning, "Who has it and who hasn't? Who's in and who's out?" The answer he wished for was, "We, them," or, better still, "I, them," thus presenting us with a prescription for tyranny.

Sixty years ago, in the sands of the desert, an inscription was discovered which reads, "Here am I, Captain of a Legion of Rome who served in the Libyan desert and learns and ponders this truth—there are in life but two things, love and power, and no one has both."

Is the Roman captain right when he tells us that the only choice we have is between loveless power and powerless love? The two great religious festivals of December would seem to confirm his judgment. Hanukkah, the Festival of Lights, began in darkness, in the ruthless massacre of a thousand defenseless Jews by Antiochus Epiphanes of Syria. And Christmas, which announces good tidings of great joy, began with a voice of lamentation in Ramah: Rachel weeping for her children, slaughtered by Herod the King.

And so it has continued—powerless love at the mercy of loveless power that shows no mercy; "We, them"; "I, them"; Antiochus Epiphanes and the Hasidim; Herod and the babies of Bethlehem; Adolf Hitler and the Holocaust; Joseph Stalin and the Gulag; Saddam Hussein and the Kurds; and on, and on, and on . . .

This vulnerability of love and goodness continues to find expression in our celebrations at Hanukkah and Christmas; for the Hanukkah candle is lit, and the Hanukkah candles will continue to shine against the encroaching darkness; while our Christmas carols sing tenderly of a young girl, homeless in a bitter wind and a bleak winter, whose little infant son was satisfied with a stable, a breastful of milk, and a manger full of hay.

132

The interesting thing to notice about the Roman soldier, the English lord, and the Russian revolutionary is that for all their differences, they are unanimous in their view that power cannot be separated from character nor understood apart from it. The Roman tells us that power forces character to choose, the Englishman warns us that power will corrupt and may even destroy our character, while the Russian demonstrates that the exercise of power reveals our character. With one voice they declare that the nature of our power is determined by the content of our character. The exercise of power is never merely a matter of how much strength, might, and energy we possess, but of the values we cherish, the loyalties we serve, and what we wish to accomplish.

This brings us very close indeed to a definition of power. I'm going to risk one by saying that power is the ability to achieve purpose, the ability to accomplish what we wish to achieve. But because wishes and purposes are expressions of the self, the vital part of personality, power is not merely what we have the means to accomplish, but what our character will allow us to accomplish.

There's a revealing story told of a Scottish Covenanter, charged with treason and hauled before an English king who asked him imperiously, "Do you not know that it is within my power to release you?" To which the canny Scot, who already reckoned himself a dead man, replied, "Your Majesty, it may be within your power, but it's no' within your nature!"

There are many things within our power that are not within our nature. If you will forgive an Irish way of putting it, there are many things we could do except that we couldn't do them! I am physically strong enough to injure a child. But the very thought of it, even to mention it in the way I am now speaking of it, is abhorrent to me. I cringe at the thought of it. To use my power in that way would be to offend every value I honor, and every ideal I admire, and every image of myself I have ever cherished.

Notice also that if power is the ability to achieve our purpose, then sometimes it will look like weakness. Accomplishing our purpose may require, not strength and forcefulness, but patience, restraint—passivity, even. And these qualities are often interpreted, or misinterpreted, as signs of weakness, not expressions of power. Yet this will not disturb us so long as we remember that even though forcefulness and aggressiveness look powerful, they are really expressions of weakness if they cannot accomplish what we wish them to do.

There was an excellent example of what I mean in the obituary of James Reston, former executive editor of *The New York Times*, thought by some to be the most influential journalist of this generation. Mr. Reston greatly admired Jean Monet, the French visionary, and loved to quote and put into practice a saying of his hero, "If you don't demand credit for things, you can push them through."

So it was that at times James Reston was well content to make himself invisible, to become "the silent mover of the play," satisfied to remain unacknowledged so long as his ends were achieved. This leads me to say: Before you do anything, always ask yourself, "Now, what do I really wish to accomplish?" and then, "How can I accomplish it?"

This brings us to one of the most searching questions of all, one that pierces to the thoughts and purposes of the heart: "How am I in my place of power?"

We all have a place of power, though not all of us may realize that we do. Sometimes it comes from having a pretty face, a pleasing form, brains, children, eloquence, love, money, influence, or fame. How are we in our place of power, and how does our character express itself in shaping, refining, and elevating our use of it?

Are we long-suffering or insufferable, patient or petulant? Do we explain or do we explode? Are we tender or tyrannical, cruel

134   *The Fine Art of Being Imperfect*

or courteous, respectful or ruthless, merciful or merciless, forgiving or ferocious? Do we laugh with people or only at them?

The real test of character, you see, is not how we behave toward those who have power over us, but how we behave toward those over whom we have power: not how we deal with our boss, but how we treat our secretary; not how obsequious we are to the president of the company, but what our attitude is to the waitress in the company cafeteria. Bullies are adept at finding the right boots to lick, and at kicking those who dare not strike back. That's why they are contemptible. Cowards are savage when dealing with the helpless, and servile when seeking to please the powerful. One might say that their abuse of power does not so much reveal their character as display their lack of it. How do you treat people you don't need?

This brings us to the most important question of all: How is God in His place of power?

What are we to make of it when the Christmas choirs burst into the "Hallelujah Chorus," affirming with every stretched instrument and strained voice that "the Lord God Omnipotent reigneth"? If the universal abuse of power has occasioned a universal suspicion of it, we should hardly expect omnipotence to escape unscathed. If the trouble with power is that we find it hard to trust, then surely the trouble with omnipotence is that it seems impossible to love, for it overwhelms us and we miss its heart of kindness. We are told that God is love, but His tenderness is lost in His power, and His mercy in His might. So we find it easier to fear Him than to trust Him, and too easily allow ourselves to settle into an attitude of grievance, resentment, and hostility. We are afraid that even His bounty is a cloak for some more sinister intention, and we will allow ourselves to trust neither His goodness nor our own happiness. No one saw this more clearly or expressed it more forcefully than Herman Melville. In *Moby Dick,* Captain Ahab sees his ship held in a violent storm, illumined from bow to stern in a supernatural light, and screams his opposition to the Source of it:

> I know Thee, Thou clear Spirit, and I know that Thy proper worship is defiance! Come to me as Power and there is that here which to the last gasp of this earthquake life will resist Thee. . . .

What we fail to realize is that God's power is the expression of His character and cannot be separated from it. His omnipotence is the instrument of His love, so that His power may be called power only because it accomplishes His good and loving purpose. God's omnipotence declares that we do not have to choose between loveless power and powerless love, for His every act reveals and expresses the power of love.

Always there were those who required a show of power: "Rend the heavens and come down!" they cried. But when He did He took most of them by surprise, as George MacDonald expresses in "That Holy Thing":

> They all were looking for a king
> To slay their foes and lift them high;
> Thou cam'st a little baby thing
> That made a woman cry.

"Thy mighty arm lay bare!" they demanded. But when He not only made bare His mighty arm but showed them His even mightier heart, it was in a thirty-two-year-old Jewish carpenter whose own loving arms were nailed fast by the loveless power of Imperial Rome. How weak and foolish it all seemed!

Yet the weakness of God is stronger than humankind, and the foolishness of God wiser than our wisdom. For in these acts of seemingly powerless love, God brought omnipotence to bear on human pride, folly, and estrangement. In them He loved us into

The Fine Art of Being Imperfect

loving, and smiled us into smiling, and forgave us into repentance, and called us home to Himself.

For what are we to do with an omnipotence that not only holds the world in its hands, but lays itself in a mother's arms; that refuses to negotiate except from weakness; that is so afraid of overwhelming us that sometimes we can't even find it; that so disguises itself that we fail even to recognize Him who refuses to put His name on anything and whose voice is heard, not in the thunder of His power, but in a baby's whimper and a young man's cry of dereliction? This is an omnipotence not only worthy of our trust, but deserving of our love, adoration, and obedience.

Once again, nobody saw this more clearly or expressed it more powerfully than Melville. Let me finish Captain Ahab's speech:

> I know Thee, Thou clear Spirit, and I know that Thy proper worship is defiance! Come to me as Power and there is that here which to last gasp of this earthquake life will resist Thee. But come in Thy lowest form of love, and I will kneel and kiss Thee.

21

YES, NO,
AND NEVERTHELESS

Have you learned to say Nevertheless?

Karl Barth, one of the most influential theologians of our time, tells us that when his grandson was learning to talk, his first word was Yes. He said it in German, which is easier than saying it in English. *Ja* sounds a bit like Mamma, babba, Dadda, or *Abba*, the Hebrew word for father—all of them good words to learn on.

Flushed with his success, the little fellow said Yes to everything. "It was," said Barth, "a distinctively intense and friendly Yes." Indeed, it sounded to the grandfather-theologian like a faint recollection of the great Yes, the Divine Yes, spoken by God when He had finished His work of Creation and pronounced it "very good," so that "the morning stars sang together, and all the sons of God shouted for joy."

The child's Yes invites us to be childlike, not only by affirming the world but by trusting it. His word expresses the assurance, learned from his mother's eyes and his father's face, that whatever should go wrong, everything would be all right. The heart of childlikeness is not, as we so often suppose, innocence, but a trustfulness that refuses to take the world in fear. It sees a face of reassuring love bending over our terror, and God's Spirit brooding like a dove over the world of His making with warm breast and—ah!—bright wings.

To say Yes in this way is to espouse a religious humanism that rejoices in all things human and celebrates the creativity of the human spirit. It is to have the eyes of our eyes opened, not only to see the world, but to perceive it charged with the grandeur of God. It is to enjoy the world aright by remembering how lately we were made and how wonderful it was when we came into it.

Having told us that his little grandson's indiscriminate Yes is a recollection of the Divine Yes, Barth next wants us to know how dissimilar they are, for God's Yes always has a No in it. The little boy was not to be blamed for this, for, truth to tell, his mother had enough Nos for both of them. I heard of a youngster once who, when asked his name, replied, "My name is John Don't."

We say No to our children to protect them from harm, for they have not yet discovered that water will certainly wet, and fire will surely burn. God's No to us may be necessary for our survival: it is certainly essential to our identity, to our knowing who we are. To define means to say No to some possibilities. Definition is the line between what we are and what we are not. We define ourselves by choosing the limits of our nature. If there isn't anything we wouldn't do, we have no character. If we are capable of anything, we cease even to be human and sink to the level of beasts. The first casualty of a humanism that recognizes no limits and exercises no restraint is our humanity. Chesterton got it right: Art and morality have this in common, that they both know where to draw the line.

Yet we complain when God teaches us to draw the line. We begin to think of Him as we thought of our parents when we resented their discipline and accused them of spoiling our fun. God thus becomes the great killjoy whose "Thou shalt not!" limits our freedom and ruins our sport. It seems never to occur to us that it is this setting of limits that gives shape to our person and makes our freedom possible.

The lines that mark the tennis court, and the net that interrupts so many of our best shots, may seem a bit of a nuisance; but if we dispense with them we haven't enhanced our skill and enlarged our freedom, we have made tennis impossible. We haven't improved our game; we no longer have a game.

In a similar way, it may appear irksome to study the depth of the water, the location of sandbars and the configuration of reefs, but if we wish to enjoy the freedom of the seas we must submit to the discipline of chart and compass. This may seem to impose an unhappy restraint, but it is really the gift of voyage.

There is another reason why our Yes should have a No in it, why it is not enough simply to affirm the goodness of Creation: It is the need to acknowledge the troubles that afflict us, the sadness that belongs to the human condition. We need to recognize the futility, the anti-meaning, the sense of forsakenness and despair which are part of the intellectual and spiritual atmosphere in which we live and which threatens to demoralize and overwhelm us with its melancholy.

Indeed, we must go even further to acknowledge the No that is the limit of life itself, the negation that is our mortality, the death that has become the dirty little secret that sex used to be. This No is so menacing that, as Freud tells us, we falsify our life by refusing to think about it until it is upon us, wiping us out, destroying all that we are and everything we have hoped for. We may express it by saying that our life is finished, or that it is an unfinishedness. It is all the same, for however we put it, we can't live with it. Camus tells us that we hate death because it makes the lie definitive—the lie that we have endless time in which to improve our mind, reconcile our relationships, make our character, and complete our work.

Do you remember Lear's words to his beloved Cordelia who is dead? Why, the foolish, fond old man will crack the vaults of heaven with his grief, for Cordelia is gone forever:

The Fine Art of Being Imperfect

> Thou'lt come no more,
> Never, never, never,
> never, never.

The words are like a bell tolling the funeral of life and joy and love and hope. This is the No, the Never that marks the limit of everything.

How are we to deal with this No? One way is by acceptance, by resigning and reconciling ourselves to the fact of it. Hesketh Pearson, dear and good friend of Malcolm Muggeridge, distressed by the thought of his own mortality, wandered one day into an English country cemetery and was immensely comforted to read the serene words from *Cymbeline,* which most happily throw off the fretfulness, pain, and injustice of this world:

> Fear no more the heat o' the sun,
> Nor the furious winter's rages;
> Thou thy worldly task hast done,
> Home art gone and ta'en thy wages . . .
>
> Fear no more the frown o' the great,
> Thou art past the tyrant's stroke . . .
>
> Quiet consummation have,
> And renowned be thy grave!

Others are not content with quiet consummation. When Dylan Thomas considered his own father's unfulfilled life, he thought that

> Old age should burn and rave at close of day;
> Rage, rage against the dying of the light.

Yet in another mood Thomas tells us that death wins no victory, for "Though lovers be lost, love shall not, and death shall have no dominion." He is really whistling in the dark in this brave and noble poem, for if lovers be lost then love is lost. There is no love but that which lovers know, and if they perish, their love perishes with them.

The poet's words were of little comfort to his wife Caitlin. When Thomas died in St. Vincent's Hospital in New York City, the staff had to put her in a straitjacket, so unrestrained was her grief; and when she came to write about it, she called her book *Leftover Life to Kill*. It tells us all that if lovers be lost, death has dominion enough.

There are those who say that our desire for immortal life is sheer selfishness, undisguised conceit, naked egotism. But it is not egotism that cries out for it, but love. Loving you as I do, how can I bear to lose you, or consider it anything but an outrage against all reason that one so lovely, so wise, and so honest should be lost?

It is here that Barth helps us again by pointing out a second difference between his little grandson's Yes and the Divine Yes. It is that God's Yes is really a Nevertheless. Barth tells us why. He says that every day is a day of darkness, of death; a day of merited and unmerited suffering; a day of devils and demons. All this is true, he says, but it is not decisive; for every day is also a day of God's life in us, and presence with us, and love for us.

Every life needs a Nevertheless. Some of us need to say it about our career, or our relationships, or our character. All our failures call for a Nevertheless, and if we can say it, they will not add up to failure. Our Nevertheless can help us face down the appalling memories that assail us in the wee small hours of the morning. It reminds us that the tribulations through which we pass need speak no final word, for in everything God cooperates for good with those who love Him.

We need to say Nevertheless, not only about our life, but about our death and about the death of those who are dear to us. Sir James Simpson discovered chloroform; that was his life's accomplishment. His life's sorrow was that he lost his little girl. She is buried in Edinburgh, with a lump of granite to mark the spot. And on the granite is her name, and her dates, with that pitifully short time between them, and the word "Nevertheless." The promise of eternal life is God's Nevertheless hurled against the arrogance of our mortality.

James Dickie once wrote a book called *God's Images* and filled it, not only with fine words, but with imaginative drawings. He dedicated it to the woman he loved, and lost to death, with these poignantly beautiful words:

> God bless you, my good girl.
> Bride of the first night.
> Now of the first Light.

Our Nevertheless is often spoken, but it is sometimes danced or played. In Jerusalem, just as "Desert Shield" became "Desert Storm," Zubin Mehta was conducting the Israel Philharmonic Orchestra, with Isaac Stern as soloist. The sirens sounded, warning that a SCUD missle was on its way. If it was not intercepted, it would certainly explode, perhaps to release poison gas or germs. The members of the audience put on their gas masks, and the orchestra left the stage. "Then," said *The New York Times,* "with awesome courage" Isaac Stern returned, and played Bach's *Sarabande for Solo Violin,* affirming the triumph of civilization and order over chaos and death.

Bach's is not the only music to do so. Beethoven's *Fidelio* is the composer's thrilling Nevertheless flung in the face of all tyranny in every age. And so is Mozart's music. Karl Barth loved Mozart. He said that when the angels are about their official business of praising God they sing Bach; but when God gives them the afternoon off, they go home to their families whistling Mozart. He tells us that Mozart's music makes audible both light and dark, joy and sorrow, life and death. Yet it always moves, so that light increases and the shadows fall without disappearing. Joy overtakes sorrow without extinguishing it, and Yes rings out louder than the ever-present No. This is the music's "Trimphant Charm," its consolation and its gift of hope.

One day, when my darling Jennifer was a little girl, filled with eagerness she came into the living room to ask me a question. I was listening to music at the time. Having answered her, I said, "Jennifer, music is playing. Why aren't you dancing?" And Jennifer, who was so ethereal it seemed her feet hardly ever touched the ground, danced her way back to her friends.

Zorba the Greek taught the Englishman to dance, and there on the seashore they danced splendidly, not because life is perfect, but because it is good; not because it is just, but because it is joyous; not because they were saints, but because they had found grace. Thus they danced their Nevertheless.

The Fine Art of Being Imperfect